# Ven

Revised, reedited... ...eased through Kindle Direct
Publishing on March 6, 2011

And revised and tweaked again March 31, 2012

Finally revised for paper in May 2015

(Originally released April 26, 2003)

For more information about the author, please visit
www.billsnow.com

Cover designed by Amber Cordova,
www.ambercordova.com

## If you are...

... an entrepreneur

... an early stage or first time entrepreneur

... a "wannabe" entrepreneur

... thinking about starting a business

... thinking about raising money

... thinking about wading into the world of venture capital

And if you find yourself full of more questions than answers.

Then this is your no nonsense guide to cutting through the clutter in the venture capital world. Find value, find reality, and get a kick in the pants.

## Legal Mumbo Jumbo

# Venture Capital 101

## -- Contents --

# About Bill Snow

 Bill Snow is an investment banker, writer, speaker, observer, kinesthetic learner, M&A expert, music lover, and deal closer. He learns by doing then by writing about it. You can contact Bill at bill@billsnow.com or visit him at his website www.billsnow.com. You can also utilize the sundry social media sites below...

Facebook: https://www.facebook.com/BillSnowFanPage

LinkedIn: http://www.linkedin.com/in/billsnow

Twitter: http://www.twitter.com/bill_snow

## Books by Bill Snow

*Venture Capital 101*

*Mergers & Acquisitions For Dummies*

*Networking Is A Curable Condition*

# Special Introduction For The Revised Versions

Wow. Where did twelve years go? I released *Venture Capital 101* in the spring of 2003 by giving it away for free on my website, and now twelve years later, I am releasing it (finally!) on paper. And the electronic version is also being updated. I hope you enjoy it and find it helpful and useful.

I wrote this book shortly after losing an opportunity to raise some capital for a company. The chairman of the company pointedly asked me, "What the heck do you know about venture capital?" Well, the expletive he used wasn't "heck." So I started writing and less than a month later I finished *Venture Capital 101.*

Initially, I circulated it for free. After one too many people told me, "you should sell that!" I decided to sell it. In fact, I set up a website with a partner and we sold *Venture Capital 101* along with some other entrepreneurial products and resources. Eventually, that website ran its course and we closed it.

Please keep in mind I originally wrote this book in the years immediately following the dotcom crash. While I have updated some of the industry data for this version of the book, other references seem slightly outdated. That said, the basic lessons of *Venture Capital 101* are as relevant and applicable today as they were in the aftermath of the dotcom crash.

To inject a little humor and irreverence, I decided to memorialize my black lab, Iggy, by naming the fictional venture capital firm after him. For a further dose of irreverence, I decided to make other pop culture references, including the Rolling Stones, Husker Du, the Rat Pack, Alice Cooper, and Led Zeppelin.

The fictional startup company, "Black Dog Enterprises," can either be a reference to the Zeppelin tune "Black Dog" or to the fact my dog, Iggy, was in fact, a black dog. I'll leave it to the reader to decide. I even referenced a Keith Richards' guitar tuning (which I think I didn't quite get right), which I cheekily claimed was a paradigm for venture capital.

Twelve years later, the dog, Iggy (pictured nearby) is no longer with us. He died on October 23, 2010 at the age of fourteen. Keith Richards, of course, is still with us, as is Iggy Pop, the namesake of my late, great, black dog.

I eventually left the startup and venture capital world behind as I began to work with larger and more established companies. Through the magic of the Internet, *Venture Capital 101* wound up on the desk of someone at Wiley Publishing and I got book deal to write *Mergers & Acquisitions For Dummies.* The people who publish those "For Dummies" books like irreverence. Funny how that works.

And all because I was a bit miffed at losing some business in the spring of 2003.

-Bill Snow, Chicago, IL, January 23, 2011 and revised on May 17, 2015

# Preface

As the title of this document suggests, Venture Capital 101 is an introductory look into the world of venture capital. It is intended to bridge the oft-large knowledge chasm between those "in the know" and those who aspire to entrepreneurship, and as such, this "entry level course" should not be construed as a 300, 500, or graduate level class.

I do not expect Venture Capital 101 to be a revelation for venture capitalists (VCs) and experienced entrepreneurs. Instead, I hope those experienced parties simply nod their heads in agreement with what this document reveals. Pumping their fists in the air and exclaiming, "Yes! It's about time someone wrote this!" would be great, but nods will suffice.

Venture Capital 101, I hope, will be a revelation of sorts for both wannabe entrepreneurs and early stage entrepreneurs.

Earlier in my career, I spent time trying to obtain venture capital financing for a couple of different endeavors. I look back in horror as I realize the multitude and depth of my mistakes. The approach, the timing, the understanding, and above all, the strength of the opportunities were all wrong and weak. Frankly, I was clueless.

The big challenge I faced during my learning process was the lack of information. I slowly learned the venture capital world seemed to contain some universally accepted maxims, but these truths, phrases, and decorum were not readily available, especially in the days prior to the Internet. While I eventually learned, my education was very much trial and error, with the emphasis on error.

As my career segued into the investment-banking world and I reviewed hundreds, if not thousands, of business plans, I realized that I was not alone in my errors. The same myths, the same misconnections, and the same errors were being played out in front of me on a daily basis. Simply, people were wasting huge amounts of time and money chasing venture capital for deals that were either too early stage for venture capital, or worse, never had a chance of obtaining venture capital.

Venture Capital 101 evolved from a series of presentations I gave at Chicago-area universities, from numerous meetings (impromptu and planned) I had with entrepreneurs, and from numerous articles I wrote for various websites and on-line resources. I created this document as a means of providing the type of information I wish I had entrée to years ago.

From my first hand experience I can attest to the enormous gap between perceptions and reality. Frankly, I have dealt with plenty of clueless venture capital seeking entrepreneurs. I created Venture Capital 101 with a certain élan because I wanted to impart this information to laypeople in a style imbued with humor, directness, and a little irreverence thrown in for good measure.

## Goals for Venture Capital 101

First and foremost, I hope this book helps dispel the many myths and misconceptions about venture capital. Next, I hope this book helps to better position entrepreneurs for successful venture capital raises by identifying the characteristics venture capitalists find attractive and by providing a framework for when and how to raise venture capital.

Also, I hope the book demonstrates venture capital is not a stamp of approval. You can build a successful company without raising venture capital. In other words, aspiring to build a company that is not "venture worthy" is not a shameful act. Lastly, I hope the book shows the reader that "cutting bait" and dumping bad ideas is a perfectly acceptable alternative to wasting time and money chasing venture capital for deals that are not venture worthy.

# A Series of Doors

Venture capital is much like life: a series of doors. You cannot open any of the doors. Someone on the other side must open the door for you in order for you to pass through. To get someone to open a door you have to present yourself (or your business plan) in the best light possible. If someone else is doing a better job than you, the door will open for your competitor and stay closed for you. If the person behind the door likes you better than all the others, the door will open for you, and the process is repeated.

Talk to the minor league baseball player who never made the big leagues. Talk to the undrafted free agent football player who was cut on the last day of training camp. They understand the door analogy.

As much as they wanted to move to the next level that last door was not opened for them. Some people view these obstructions as "walls" or "ceilings" – objects impossible to pass through. In reality, every wall or ceiling is a door that can be opened for you, if only you know how to present yourself.

Venture capital is the same: The power in this game lies in the hands of those who have the money. It is up to the entrepreneur to present himself or herself in the best possible light, to out-work, out-plan, and out-prepare all competition and become the best option on the VC's doorstep. Only then might the door be opened for the entrepreneur.

## Fairness?

The process isn't "fair" because, like it or not, entrepreneurs need VCs more than VCs need entrepreneurs. If you don't like this basic premise, you don't have to play. This is a free society (not a "fair" society) and you can opt out. If you're looking for fairness and compassion, talk to your mother. If you're looking for egalitarianism, hang out at a Phish concert and join Greenpeace.

Fairness is only fair to the person making the rules. In other words, "fairness" is arbitrary. If you want to be in the for-profit world you should eschew notions of fairness. When two parties freely enter into an agreement, arbitrariness is not involved: Terms are offered, terms are accepted. If the first party does not like the deal, no terms are offered. If the second party doesn't like the terms, the terms are rejected. Fairness is a term that you should reject if you choose to seek venture capital.

## Usury

To get money, you have to prove you can make money for others. Your plan will be nitpicked, your financial assumptions ground through the grinder, and you will be personally criticized. You better have thick skin.

## Use of Terms

Venture Capital 101 uses the acronym "VC" interchangeably when referring to both people (venture capitalists) and an industry (the venture capital industry). I hope this does not cause any confusion.

## Thanks Are In Order

I'd like to thank a few people: Len Batterson and Bob Cross from my Vcapital days; Bob Geras for his expert advice and "take no prisoners" opinion; Vic Pascucci, the TannedFeet.com impresario; Dr. Harold Welsch of DePaul's Entrepreneurship Program; Joe Mallugen from Movie Gallery; Steve "separate the issues" Eich from Steppenwolf Theater; and Andrea Heilman for her help with editing and proofreading. Any typo or error found in this document is my fault, not Andrea's fault!

And most importantly, to my mother, Carol Snow, who always provided love, support, and great cooking; and to my father, the original (albeit shorter) Bill Snow, who generated pearls of wisdom with such ease and consistency that he often forgot he was the one who originally coined many (but not all) of the brilliant terms I now pass off as my own.

## On With the Show

I hope you find Venture Capital 101 to be a useful and helpful guide and teacher. Go forth and follow your dream.

-Bill Snow, Chicago, IL, April 2003

# Lesson 1: Venture Capital 101

Early stage entrepreneurs face three main challenges: money, money, and money. In addition to seeking money, early stage entrepreneurs spend a large portion of their time seeking money.

VCs are often viewed as a natural stop in the quest for money. VCs obviously have plenty of money, and they're looking for the next great idea, aren't they? VCs are degenerate risk takers who are looking for the next Microsoft, aren't they? VCs will take a flier on unproven concepts written in crayon on scraps of paper, don't they?

The harsh answer is: No. VCs do not take risks so much as they mitigate, manage, and avoid risks. A VC, like any other investor, is looking for the highest return with the smallest risk. VCs do not fund ideas; VCs do not take fliers on unproven concepts.

And if you are looking for egalitarianism, the world of venture capital is not for you. Venture capital does not have entitlement programs. You're not going to get funded because you're you.

## Sense of Entitlement + Bitter Reality = Many Wasted Steps

A "how to be a better golfer" joke made the Internet rounds a few years ago. The number one suggestion was, "if you want to be a better golfer, go back and start at an earlier age."

The lesson is similar lesson for many entrepreneurs trying to raise funds in the difficult post 9/11 market: "If you want to get venture capital funding, go back and be a better entrepreneur."

The bitter reality aspirant entrepreneurs need to face is that VCs are returning money to their limited partners. While venture capital deals are graded on a very steep curve, being the best of a sub par group will not yield investment. If the choice is investing in lesser companies or returning money to investors, VCs choose the latter.

Many entrepreneurs, especially in the boom time of the late 1990's, developed a sense of entitlement where they thought if they came up with a novel enough idea, VCs would fund them, sight unseen.

The truth is VCs did not operate this way in the 90's, and they certainly do not operate this way today. A safe assumption is they will not operate this way in 2010, 2020 or at any other time in the future.

An entrepreneur who dives into the world of venture capital armed only with a misguided and unprepared sense of entitlement will meet with bitter reality, resulting in wasted steps, for both the entrepreneur and the VC.

## **Say Hello to My Little Friend...Reality**

Simply put, entrepreneurs need to be realistic; venture capital is not for everyone; they need to operate in an industry (with a product) that has the chance to become a "billion dollar baby;" they need to seek the right investors at the right time; they need to have a "hook," that is, give investors and customers a compelling reason to act (invest and buy, respectively); they must have a business that builds real assets on the balance sheet (cash); they must close deals and book sales; they must offer a solution that solves a real pain point (and not offer a solution looking for a problem); they must compile a world-class management team; and they must be imbued with persistence, doggedness, resourcefulness, and creativity.

If they achieve all of the above, maybe they'll be ready for a venture capital investment.

If you are at the "idea stage," if your company is pre-revenue, you probably don't have chance with VCs. Your company (or idea) simply does not fit their criteria.

## Venture Capital Is Not For Everyone

Not every company is a venture worthy deal. Just because VCs reject your company does not mean your company is a "bad" company. It just means it doesn't fit within the very narrow requirements of the VC industry.

Venture capital isn't the only way to grow a business. A small discount retailer in Arkansas and a milkshake mixer salesman turned restaurateur in suburban Chicago built large companies without venture capital. They developed or created a model that worked, made a profit, and replicated that model over and over. Today, you can buy shares of either company under the tickers WMT and MCD.

## Billion Dollar Babies

Size and speed matter: VCs want their investments to grow large and do so quickly. Since VCs typically look for returns ranging from 5 to 20 times their investment, the portfolio company needs to obtain market capitalization measured in the hundreds of millions of dollars, or better still, in the billions of dollars. To support this kind of capitalization, the portfolio company needs revenues measured in (at least) the hundreds of millions of dollars.

Every company has what I call a "revenue ceiling." The entrepreneur has to ask the tough question: "Is my baby a billion dollar company, or is it a nice $10 million dollar a year business?" Running a $10 million a year business is fine, nothing wrong with that revenue size, but if the company is limited to a relatively modest revenue amount, that company will not be able to raise money from VCs.

## Utilize the Right Investors at the Right Time

VCs do not fund pipe dreams. The "F's" - friends, family (and fools) fund pipe dreams. VCs do not fund start-ups. If you are lucky, angels fund start-ups. VCs fund existing companies.

## Have a Hook

Entrepreneurs need to give investors and customers a compelling reason to act (invest and buy, respectively). A great technology that does not solve a pressing problem will not sell. A mediocre technology that cures an ill will sell.

This is another tough question entrepreneurs must ask of themselves, because everyone believes his/her widget, process, or technology is exactly what the world needs. The truth is, unless you fix a pressing problem, you are nothing more than a solution looking for a problem. If you don't have a headache, would you be willing to pay 10 bucks for world's greatest headache cure? Would you pay 10 cents? Of course not.

## Build Assets

A VC will only be interested in your deal if your proposition has a clear path to revenue and profitability. If you are asking for a VC investment to help you prove the model or develop the science, don't waste your time. This means you a looking for money to merely pay your salary. While your salary builds value for you, it does not necessarily build value for the VC.

You must be able to prove that your company will use the investment to expand production, marketing, and/or acquire other assets that will allow it to build even more assets on the balance sheet.

## Close Deals and Book Sales

Simply put, if your company has not yet booked sales, and in most cases, substantial sales, then you face a very difficult time trying to raise venture capital. VCs require market acceptance, and the proof of concept used for this test is called actual sales.

## Solve a Real Pain Point

Does your product solve a real problem or is your product a solution in search of a problem? Entrepreneurs need to conduct market research. Gut instinct may not be enough.

## World-Class Management

One person cannot do everything. A venture worthy business will have experienced executives on the team, people who "have been there, done that." This means a CEO, CFO, COO, and VP of Sales who have all worked for large successful companies, and preferably successful start ups, too. Your team needs to have experience building value and exiting successfully.

## Have Persistence, Doggedness, Resourcefulness, and Creativity

Please note the lack of the word "stupidity" in the above header. It is one thing to pursue your dream with relentless abandon; it is another thing to flog a dead horse.

## Speak Venture Capital Lingo

Don't look like a deer caught in the headlights when people start talking about angel investors, "A" rounds, authorized shares, and so on.

## Get In the Game

If you think you want to play the game, the game starts by getting in. If you don't yet have a company (or an idea, for that matter) and if you lack entrepreneurial experience, I recommend quitting your current dead end job and finding employment with an entrepreneur/startup company. You will learn most quickly by actually doing and experiencing. Don't put yourself above a job. Be willing to work for free (or for equity) for a period of time in order to prove your value. Think of it as an investment in yourself.

If you have an idea that you think you can build into a sizable company, stop thinking about it and do it. You can't win if you're not in the game. Organize a corporation, hire an attorney to draft stock purchase agreements, sink your life savings into it, take out second mortgage, recruit partners who can help you execute your plan and realize your dream, work your rear off, be ready to wheel and deal, and prepare yourself for long hours every day and compromise at every turn.

## Onward and Upward

If I haven't scared you away, let's take a look at this thing called venture capital.

# Lesson 2: What Is Venture Capital?

A venture capital fund is a pool of money that accepts a higher level of risk in exchange for higher returns. A venture capitalist is a person who works at a venture capital fund. The fund makes investments in (predominately) privately held growth companies. The VC may or may not be playing with his/her own money.

A venture capital firm is actually comprised of two entities (the fund and the management company) and two players (limited partners or LPs and general partners or GPs). The LPs are the investors. They buy pieces of the fund, which are called membership units. The GPs are the venture capitalists. They invest the fund's money in deals that meet the fund's criteria.

The fund is set up as a limited liability corporation (LLC), which affords the LPs protection in the event something goes wrong with an investment. The GPs run some risk of being involved in a lawsuit, because they are actively managing the day-to-day operation of the fund. The LPs are passive investors, and therefore shielded from liability.

This is an important distinction when you consider that most LPs have substantial funds, and any one investment in a particular venture fund will likely be a small portion of their total holdings. Imagine how quickly VC investing would dry up if a person involved in a lawsuit against a portfolio company could also go after the deep-pocketed limited partners!

In setting up the fund, the GPs will determine the following: life, size, and investment criteria. The LPs are protected from dilution because the fund is "capped" at a certain amount. If an LP invests $5 million in a $20 million fund, that LP will own 25% of the fund.

Should the VCs find investors willing to invest amounts over the cap, they may elect to start a second fund, but they will not be able to add this money into the existing fund. The fund typically has a finite life, usually 10 years, after which the LPs hope/plan to get their original investment back, plus some appreciation.

The fund pays a management fee (usually 2% to 3%) to the management company. This fee is usually collected only in the early years of the fund when most of the fund is still flush with cash. The management company employs VCs, as well as a support staff.

In addition to salaries, the management fee is used to take care of the other associated costs: rent, insurance, utilities, office supplies, travel, and so on. The venture capitalists may or may not be limited partners (hence, they may or may not be playing with their own money).

Investments are made in companies (called portfolio companies) that meet the fund's criteria. The hope is the portfolio companies will grow rapidly, create value, and either go public or become acquired by public companies. This is called a "liquidity event."

After returning the original investment to the LPs, the GPs and LPs will split the remainder (called the carry) at a previously agreed upon rate. This rate is usually 80-20, that is, eighty percent to the LPs and twenty percent to the GPs.

### *Extra Credit Reading: What is a PIPE?*

*Some funds make investments in public companies. This is called a PIPE (private investment in public entity). This form of investment gained in popularity following the aftermath of the 1990's stock bubble. Investing in public companies gives venture capitalists liquidly.*

### **Iggy Ventures: An Example**

To create a better explanation, let's create a fictional venture capital fund. First, we set up two entities, Iggy Ventures, LLC (the fund) and Iggy Venture Management, LLC (the management company).

The GPs decide they will raise $100 million and make investments in the burgeoning field of Labrador retriever cleaning products. Anyone who has ever owned a black lab knows how often you have to clean those animals.

Because Iggy Ventures' GPs are very smart and well connected, they are able to raise $100 million from an assortment of limited partners. In Iggy Ventures' case, these limited partners include:

- $32 million from a very wealthy local business magnate
- $20 million from a state pension fund
- $15 million from University Endowment
- $13 million from a union pension fund
- $12 million from Iggy Ventures' GPs
- $8 million from a very wealthy basketball player

Once the money has been raised, the fund is "closed," meaning no addition funds will be added. Because the fund is a limited liability corporation (LLC), no shares are issued. Instead, each LP owns a percentage, frequently called membership units. In this example, the business magnate owns 32%, the state pension fund owns 20%, the university owns 15%, the union pension fund owns 13%, the GPs own 12%, and the basketball player owns 8%.

### *Extra Credit Reading: Diversification*

*Iggy Ventures' LPs probably will not have a majority of their holdings in Iggy Ventures. Instead, each of the LPs is using the investment in Iggy Ventures as a means to diversify his/her holdings.*

*In addition to being investors in venture funds such as Iggy Ventures, all or most of the LPs probably have their holdings spread out in a variety of financial instruments, including (but not limited to): money market accounts, real estate, blue chip stocks, mid cap stocks, micro cap stocks, corporate bonds, municipal bonds, antiques, collectibles, art, and so on.*

## Making Investments

Once the money has been raised (and the fund closed), the GPs begin to make investments per the fund's criteria. This is an important aspect for entrepreneurs to remember. GPs are bound by the covenants of the operating agreement.

The LPs invest in the fund because they believe the GPs will make wise choices with the money, but they also invest because they like/approve/are turned on by the types of investments the fund will make.

If the GPs tell the LPs the fund will invest in drug discovery and medical device deals, the LPs do not want to discover that the GPs actually invested the money in, say, a pizza parlor. Owning a pizza parlor is a perfectly honorable business, of course, but that pizza parlor will not offer the type of growth prospects offered by software, nanotech, or biotech companies.

Furthermore, LPs quite often have some professional connection or personal interest with the fund's targeted investment types. For example, the LPs of a fund that invests in medical devices and drug discovery are likely to be doctors. Doctors understand the science of the underlying investments, and if a portfolio company's drug or device becomes FDA approved, the doctors may actually use the drug or device in their work.

### *Extra Credit Reading: What Venture Capital is not*

*Venture capital is not funny money and it does not represent money that can be thrown away. Seeking venture capital effectively means you are seeking money that is earmarked for retirement pensions and college scholarships.*

## The Growth Process and Harvest

Why do GPs and LPs bother with all this work? To make money...a lot of it. While some people may have secondary egalitarian reasons (for example, some environmental funds have a "duel bottom line" where they look for high returns by investing in "green" companies), the number one reason that people play the venture capital game is to make money.

Venture capitalists make money by buying shares in companies and subsequently selling those shares for more than the original investment. It's a simple game fraught with complexities.

Ostensibly, the expected period of time from investment to harvest is usually three to ten years. In reality it is "as soon as possible!"

### *Extra Credit Reading: Liquidity Events*

*Liquidity events occur during the life of the fund, not necessarily at the end of the fund's life. Money returned to the fund (following a liquidity event) does not return to the fund at the same time (for example, at the end of the fund's ten-year life). Instead, each of these portfolio companies realized a liquidity event at different times. As each liquidity event was realized, funds were disbursed to the LPs and the GPs.*

## Portfolio Company

A company that receives a venture investment is called a portfolio company. Some portfolio companies grow, others languish. During the growth phase GPs will constantly evaluate the progress of each portfolio company and determine if the company warrants additional support (money).

Some investors are active in the operations of the portfolio companies, while other investors are passive. In some funds, the GPs themselves act as advisors; while other funds (usually the larger ones with the means) employ very experienced support people.

To facilitate growth, some portfolio companies require additional investment from the fund, and others obtain investments from other funds. Some show signs of flame out relatively soon, and the VCs may decide against any further investment. The job of the VC is to mitigate, manage, and spread out risk.

## Iggy Ventures Revisited

Let's go back to our example of Iggy Ventures. The GPs made 20 investments during the first couple years of the fund's life. Ten years go by, and some of Iggy Venture's investments have borne fruit (in vary degrees), while others have died on the vine. Here's the status of Iggy Ventures' 20 portfolio companies:

- 3 three went public (with high returns on investment)
- 5 merged with or were acquired by public companies (with high returns on investment)
- 2 were sold to private investors (with medium returns on investment)
- 3 were liquidated or sold (at a loss)
- 5 went out of business (with a total loss of investment)
- 2 are zombies (the "living dead")

In the final reckoning, 13 portfolio companies (the ones that went public, merged, were acquired or sold) all returned money to the fund. In eight cases the returns were high, in two cases the returns were decent, and in three cases the returns were less than the original investment (but better than a total loss).

Five portfolio companies went out of business resulting in a total loss, and two companies became zombies, the living dead of the venture capital world. Zombies are companies that neither went out of business nor became candidates for a liquidity event. Zombies are profitable companies, therefore they do not need further investment from the fund, but zombies probably will never grow enough to yield liquidity events for their investors.

So how did Iggy Ventures do? As we recall, Iggy Ventures raised $100 million from an assortment of limited partners. A total of $300 million was returned to the fund for a profit of $200 million. Money in excess of the original investment is called the "carry," and therefore, Iggy Ventures' carry was $200 million.

Per the operating agreement, the limited partners got their original investment returned before the carry is split among the participants. Typically, LPs receive 80% of the carry and the GPs receive 20%. In the case of Iggy Ventures, the LPs split $160 million (80% of $200 million), and the GPs split $40 million (20% of $200 million).

The LPs split their share of the carry on a pro rata basis. The LP who owned 32% of the fund received 32% of the carry due to the limited partners, or $51.2 million. For this LP, the original investment of $32 million turned in $83.2 million.

The GPs split their share of the carry per some predetermined method. Senior members probably receive a larger share than junior members. And in the case of Iggy Ventures, some of the GPs invested in the fund, meaning they received pro rata share of the LPs' carry. The GPs also make money from the management fees charged in the early years of a fund's life.

## The Bottom Line

In review, what's in it for each player?

Venture Capitalists earn a management fee of 2% to 3% of the money under management and get 20% of the "carry."

Limited Partners get their initial investment back (hopefully) and then receive 80% of the carry.

25

Entrepreneurs get a chance to work their tails off and make a lot of money...for others. They obviously receive a salary (which may be under market rates), and hopefully their companies go public or are sold to public companies. Because of dilution, by the time of a liquidity event, most entrepreneurs own a small percentage of their companies (assuming they still work for the company). This is often less than 5%.

Why would entrepreneurs want venture capital? We will answer this question over the next few chapters as we examine one of Iggy Ventures portfolio companies, Black Dog Enterprises. But first, let's look the reality of venture capital.

# Lesson 3: The Reality of Venture Capital

Let's look at the numbers. As the chart on this page indicates, the venture capital world literally exploded in the mid and late 1990's. A $3 billion niche industry at the start of the decade, venture capital grew into a $100 billion industry by 2000.

Traditionally, VCs only invested in about 1,000 to 1,500 deals per year. From 1995 to 1998, VCs accelerated their investment activity, and the number of deals grew from about 2,000 per year to almost 4,000. 1999 saw over 5,500 VC investments, while 2000 saw 8,000 VC investments.

| **Amount of United States Venture Capital Investment: 1990 to 2010** | | | |
|---|---|---|---|
| Year | Investment (billions) | Number of deals | Avg. deal size (millions) |
| '90 | $2.70 | 1,471 | $1.84 |
| '91 | $2.30 | 1,279 | $1.80 |
| '92 | $3.60 | 1,415 | $2.54 |
| '93 | $3.90 | 1,209 | $3.23 |
| '94 | $4.20 | 1,239 | $3.39 |
| '95 | $7.23 | 1,864 | $3.88 |
| '96 | $10.46 | 2,601 | $4.02 |
| '97 | $14.00 | 3,201 | $4.37 |
| '98 | $19.37 | 3,694 | $5.24 |
| '99 | $50.89 | 5,556 | $9.16 |
| '00 . | $98.60 | 7,973 | $12.37 |
| '01 | $37.63 | 4,543 | $8.28 |
| '02 | $20.74 | 3,157 | $6.57 |
| '03 | $18.79 | 2,990 | $6.28 |
| '04 | $21.70 | 3,145 | $6.90 |
| '05 | $22.54 | 3,201 | $7.04 |
| '06 | $26.01 | 3,754 | $6.93 |
| '07 | $29.90 | 4,035 | $7.41 |
| '08 | $28.11 | 4,025 | $6.98 |
| '09 | $18.28 | 2,927 | $6.24 |
| '10 | $21.82 | 3,277 | $6.66 |
| *Source: PriceWaterhouseCoopers MoneyTree* | | | |

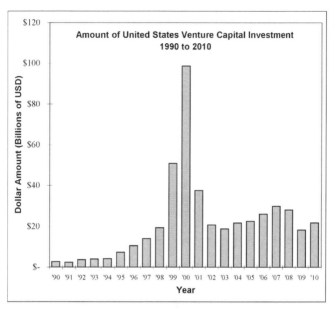

**Amount of United States Venture Capital Investment 1990 to 2010**

What fueled this growth? Books have been (and will be) written detailing the bubble economy of the late 90's and its myriad causes. An extremely abridged version will show the bubble was caused by a combination of a number of factors:

- A vibrant public market that increasingly allowed increasingly raw companies to go public.
- The buzz created by the dawning of the Internet age.
- A period of peace and prosperity.
- A manic pop culture mentality where the stock market, the Internet, start ups, and venture capital caught the fancy of the public.

While we now laugh at the dotcom era, its self absorbed gadget culture and sock puppet mascots, a more sober reading of the past decade's events is this: An industry that historically identified approximately 1,000 venture worthy companies per year suddenly identified 8,000 in a single, mad year.

Simply put, the world suddenly did not contain 7,000 more Venture worthy companies. A lot of chaff was funded, and the fallout is the stuff of legends.

Even during the mania of the late 90's, venture capital was not a large business, nor was it a common way for companies to receive funding. The fact the industry has contracted to about one fifth of its bubble peak simply means the industry is now closer to its historic and traditional size. This also means a selective industry is even more selective.

Let's put this into perspective. The United States has over 10 million companies, and size of the US economy is greater than $10 trillion. This means, in the peak venture capital year (2000), venture capital:

1. Funded less than 1 out of every 1,000 companies in the US
2. Represented less than 1% of the entire US economy

And this was in the peak year!

In 2011, the VC industry is nowhere near the size we saw in 1999-2000. Venture capital is not common, venture capital is not prevalent, venture capital is not easy to obtain, and venture capital is not for every company.

Only an extremely small number of companies will be seriously considered for venture capital, and of these, only a small percentage will actually receive a VC investment. Further, virtually none of these companies will be early stage.

## What Is An Early Stage Company And Why Don't Venture Capitalists Invest In Them?

Definitions vary depending with whom you talk, but for the purposes of Venture Capital 101, a startup refers to an early stage company, perhaps pre-incorporation. Revenues are nil, and the product is either in the idea stage or requires further development. The company is many months, if not years, away from generating revenues, let alone a profit, let alone an exit for the investors.

VCs do not invest in startups for a few simple reasons. First, risk versus reward. VCs are not degenerate risk takers, they do not invest on whim, and they are not looking to take a "flyer" on a crazy idea. They do not take on risk for risk's sake.

Instead, VCs are risk managers, which means they seek the "right" balance between risk and return ("right" being defined differently by each investor). Because VCs are looking for returns higher than the stock market traditionally offers, they are willing to take on some additional risk. Willingness to take on some additional risk does not mean a willingness to go overboard and take on all risk.

Second, in addition to risk, time plays a crucial role. The earlier the company's stage, the longer the payback time. VCs usually look to exit within three to seven years. The typical company that receives a venture capital investment has probably been around for at least three to seven years. VCs likely will be unwilling to double the exit period on an investment by investing in a startup.

Third, the earlier the company, the more handholding and babysitting will be required. While most VCs like to be involved in their portfolio investments, an early stage company may end up requiring proportionately more time than the VC would like to allot, thus decreasing the time spent working with other portfolio companies.

Finally, the size of the investment is a consideration. The startup phase usually requires less money (probably under $1 million) than later stages. While some entrepreneurs think this is an advantage (that is, "I only need $500 thousand, isn't it worth a shot in the dark for such a small amount?"), this can actually be a disadvantage.

A $500 thousand investment will require the same amount of time as a $5 million investment. Making numerous "small" investments will dilute a VC's time. Instead of making a large number of small investments, it usually makes more sense to make a small number of large investments.

### *Extra Credit Reading: Early Stage Venture Capital?*

*The cold hard fact is that venture capital funds traditionally have invested less than 1% of its funds into early stage companies.*

## <u>What Can The Early Stage Startup Do About This Reality?</u>

Become a venture worthy company! All will be revealed in future chapters as we examine "venture worthiness" and look a fictional start up company. But first, let's look at the universally accepted but unspoken maxims of venture capital

# Lesson 4: Truth, Phrases, Decorum

Early stage entrepreneurs are bound to run into a buzz saw I call the maxims of venture capital. Believe it or not, as bad as it is to run into a buzz saw, something is actually worse: Not knowing you just ran into a buzz saw.

### The Truth about Bad Ideas

- No amount of spit and polish can make a bad idea compelling. If the fundamental business model and/or underlying assumptions are faulty, a professionally prepared plan will not cure these fatal ailments.
- The "better mousetrap" theory is fatally flawed. If your target market does not have a pestilence problem, the world will not beat a path to your door to buy a "better mousetrap" they don't need.

### The Truth about Venture Capitalists

- VCs rarely say "no." They don't want to be the example a successful entrepreneur uses one day when talking about "all those idiot VCs who passed on my deal." To their credit, VCs tend to be optimistic, helpful, and encouraging. The downside of this is many entrepreneurs keep chugging on, working on bad businesses, mainly because they haven't heard, "no, not a chance in hell."
- VCs are polite people. Most people learn good manners at an early age. For example, hanging up the phone while the other person is still talking is considered impolite. No matter how irrational or long-winded the caller, most people try to end a conversation politely before hanging up the receiver. In other words, just because a VC gives you a few minutes when you call does not mean he's interested in your deal! Do not confuse good manners for interest.
- VCs utilize the "One Reason" rule. During the first step of a review process, VCs rarely read business plans: they scan them. They are not looking for reasons to invest; they are looking for reasons not to invest. They are not

looking for the singular hidden gem in your plan. Only if the plan passes this initial screening, will VCs dig deeper and seriously consider the investment.

- The entrepreneur's "greatest idea in the world" is the VC's commodity. VCs see 50, 100, 1,000 "greatest" ideas a month. Entrepreneurs need VCs more than VCs need entrepreneurs. The person who controls the money controls the situation.
- While VCs accept the fact that every investment will not turn in to a homerun, they perform their due diligence expecting every investment to be a homerun.

## **Phrases (Of Death) - Don't Say These Things**

Here are some of the sayings and phrases entrepreneurs should avoid at all costs:

*"You don't get it!"*

This is usually a sign of entrepreneurial exasperation, leveled after the entrepreneur has been rejected after the nth time. The VC probably understands more about the situation than the person leveling the charge. In fact, the exclamation is akin to yelling, "I'm telling mom!" Stop your whining and fix your plan. Or find a new job.

*"Will you sign an NDA?"*

This is a sure sign the entrepreneur is a rank amateur. In most cases, VCs find an inverse relationship between the voracity of the NDA inquiry and the quality of the deal. If your plan is based on an idea so tenuous that merely hearing what you do (or plan to do) will cause grievous harm to your plan, you don't have a plan. You have a pipe dream.

An exception to this rule is if you are far downstream with investor negotiations (for example, you've already had numerous in depth, serious, and meaningful discussions), your company actually has something proprietary, negotiations are at the "open the kimono" stage and as a result your company's secret sauce (for example, source code) is about to be revealed to the fund's technical expert. In this case, asking for a non-disclosure protection is probably appropriate.

*"These projections are conservative"*

Your rank amateur is showing! This usually means the projections are pie in the sky, and extremely unobtainable.

*"We have no competitors"*

All companies have competitors, either direct, indirect, or substitutes. Movie studios directly compete against other studios, but they also indirectly compete with every other kind of entertainment: theater, sporting events, restaurants, nightclubs, and so. Alternatives/substitutes to your product always exist. The biggest competitor you may face is apathy. The customer's decision to NOT buy your product is a possibility.

*"All we need to do is grab 1% of a $100 billion market and we'll have a billion dollar company"*

This statement is unique to exactly you...and the other 6 billion people in the world! This is yet another sign the entrepreneur is letting his rank amateur show.

*"I'll quit my job upon funding."*

This means you won't be quitting your job because you're not getting funding (from a venture capitalist). You need to make the full and complete commitment to your business long before you seek venture capital.

*"Seasoned management will be hired upon funding."*

Oh, yes! I can see the venture capitalists lining up when they read this sentence...lining up to laugh at the plan before it is condemned to the ash heap of clueless business plans.

# Basic Decorum for Entrepreneurs

Entrepreneurs looking for capital make the same set of errors with alarming regularity. Here is a list of the most common decorum mistakes:

*Give direct answers to direct questions.*

This is the number one rules violation...with a bullet! The entrepreneur is so excited about the chance to give his spiel to a decision maker that he often jumps 20 steps ahead, rushes through his answer, and generally fails to answer the question. You can almost hear the gears spinning in the entrepreneur's head as he parses every question, looking for hidden nuance and meaning in otherwise direct and clear-cut questions. Here's an example:

Q: "What are your revenues?"

A: "Our technology is portable to UNIX servers and we hope to get a patent next year after we use this venture capital round to pay back my mother."

*Be honest*

While you would think this is a basic business tenant, many entrepreneurs flat out lie about the their company and its prospects. The truth will eventually come out, don't shortchange yourself and your dream, and make sure you are honest in your presentation and answers.

One of the biggest lies entrepreneurs tell is that other investors are about to put money in the deal, and "you better get in now while you can buy at a low price."

*Be accurate*

Entrepreneurs have a tendency to gin up their companies, trying to portray their efforts and dreams in the best light possible. The combining of effort and dream seems to be the culprit here. Using the same question as posed above, here is how honesty gets twisted:

Q: "What are your revenues?"

A: "$2 million."

Sounds like a direct answer to a direct question, right? The problem, not readily apparent, is the fact that this entrepreneur doesn't have a $2 million company. He has some trailing revenue, but his $2 million figure is what he hopes the company will produce in the coming year. Make sure you have a very clear delineation between historical results and your projections.

### *Understand the lingo*

Educate yourself, do your homework, learn the terms and the language.

### *Know to whom you sent your plan*

If an investor calls you back, that investor will expect that you know the reason for the call. Saying, "huh, who are you?" is probably a bad thing! This makes it look like you are sending your plan willy-nilly to everyone and anyone. Investors usually take this as a sign that the deal has been shopped, meaning a large number of other people have passed on it.

### *Know if an investor actually invests in your type of deal*

This is a basic issue that many early stage entrepreneurs don't seem to understand. Venture capitalists' investment criteria are usually limited by their experience and/or the covenants of the fund's operating agreement.

Let's say a strong software company approaches a reputable venture capital fund that invests only in medical-related deals. The venture capitalist will likely realize this software company is a good deal, but he will refrain from investing because software is outside his area of expertise and/or the fund prohibits investment in anything other than medical device and drug discovery.

# Lesson 5: Types of Funding

Raising capital is an art, not a science. While some universal truths exist (no amount of spit and polish will make a bad idea into a compelling business plan), your chances of successfully raising capital largely deal with your preparation, your presentation, and the right source of funding at the right time.

In other words, don't take your latest brainfart to a venture capitalist and expect him to fund it. To get the attention of a VC, you need to have achieved critical mass.

### Bootstrapping

Bootstrapping means funding the company without external help. In most cases, you are investing your own money, or you are reinvesting profits (called retained earnings on your balance sheet).

Reinvesting the profits of your business back into the company can be a great way to grow your business, because you don't have to deal with external investors.

But it can also be a limiting method because odds are your company's need for growth capital will outstrip the money provided by profits. In addition to using profits, here are a couple other bootstrapping ideas:

- Use your own savings
- Take out a second mortgage
- Sell the title of your car
- Use your credit cards
- Use your creditors – delay payments on your payables and try to accelerate the collection of your receivables
- Use your customers – sell the service/product, then build it, using funds from your client
- Pre-sell your service – get the money upfront (or get an enforceable contract), then build/obtain/deliver the product

The likelihood of a company receiving investment capital without also having employed various bootstrapping methods is slim.

## Friends and Family

The first source of outside funds for many entrepreneurs usually comes from friends and family. This why you should be nice to family members – you never know when you'll have to hit them up for money. In most cases, the amount of financing from friends and family is relatively small, usually under $250,000, and in many cases under $100,000.

An entrepreneur has access to this group of people for a simple reason: They know the entrepreneur. The plus side of this kind of financing is the ease and simplicity of the deal.

Friends and family invest in a deal mainly because of the entrepreneur: they know the person, and they like the person (or at least his story of how they're all about to get rich). Friends and family typically are not sophisticated investors, often making the sell story much easier.

The down side to utilizing friends and family to finance your company is facing awkward family gatherings after you squander the investment. Ruined friendships and strained family relations are often the end result of friends and family investment.

One word of caution: Do not sell stock at high valuations as you are setting yourself up for difficult times as you try to raise money from other groups. Sophisticated investors will balk and walk if you tell them you have a $20 million valuation on your non-revenue producing company.

Conversely, if you are willing to take a haircut to obtain additional financing, uncle Stanislav may have a tough time understanding why his investment, once worth $500 a share (when he invested), is suddenly worth only 50 cents a share (when the angels invested).

# Angels and Angel Groups

Once notable milestones are met, an entrepreneur can often seek angel capital (usually $100k to $1 million). These milestones are usually revenue related, but for the purpose of contacting angels, proof of concept may be enough.

"Angels" are wealthy individuals (that is, accredited investors) who champion early stage ventures most often because they sense the ability to make a ton of money and/or they have some sort of personal interest in the company/entrepreneur.

Some angels are independent, making occasional investments when the right opportunity crosses their desks. These angels are often tough to find and usually require running in the right circles (hint: take up golf).

Working with connected service providers (accountants, lawyers, marketers, and so on) is often helpful. As you might imagine, angels often want to keep a low profile. They do not want to be inundated with boatloads of bad plans. They don't want their time wasted by haranguing entrepreneurs.

Sometimes angels form groups. Some of these groups are loose affiliations; others are organized networks. In both cases, an entrepreneur gets the ability to present the plan to the angel group, in the hopes one or more of the angels in attendance will invest.

This presentation doesn't occur until the deal has been "scrubbed" that is, reviewed, groomed, prodded and poked. Some groups charge entrepreneurs submission and presentation fees, others do not. Because the Angel group is not making a direct investment, the group is not a fund, and usually falls outside of SEC regulation.

However, your dealings with any investor may fall under the auspices of the SEC. Consult an attorney.

## Government Grants

The government will sometimes provide money in the form of grants. This grant money is for certain industries/technologies the government would like to see developed. In 2003, one of the most talked about areas is fuel cell technology.

Do your research on the Internet (http://www.governmentgrants.com), and talk to an attorney who can help you draft a grant request.

## Venture Capital Funds

As covered in Lesson 2, venture funds are limited partnerships that invest in certain types of companies.

## Debt

Small Business Administration is a federal agency that will partially guarantee bank loans to entrepreneurs. Go to http://www.sba.gov/ to learn more.

## Public Markets

VCs invest in companies that (they hope) will someday have publicly traded stock. A company with publicly traded stock affords VCs opportunity to liquidate their positions and realize (presumably) large returns. How do portfolio companies become public companies?

### *IPO*

If a company has substantial sales (usually $40 to $50 million or more), is profitable, has a few years of operating history (to provide some basis of estimating future performance), and has shown steady increases in revenue and profits, it may be able to conduct an initial public offering (IPO).

An IPO raises money from the public and then provides the buyers of the stock a market to sell (or buy) shares. The proceeds from the sale of stock go to the issuing company (minus investment banking fees of 7% to 8%). In most cases the company issues new shares, unless a founder is selling stock (which needs to be disclosed to the buying public).

In this latter case, the proceeds would flow to the founder (the seller of the stock). Common US public markets are the New York Stock Exchange (NYSE), NASDAQ, and the American Stock Exchange. A number of smaller regional exchanges exist, too.

VCs obviously want their portfolio companies to grow to the point where they can go public. An IPO usually means early investors in the company will realize a substantial return on investment.

The US only has about 15,000 publicly traded companies and even during boom times only a few hundred IPOs are conducted each year. A far more common exit is a merger with or an acquisition by a public company.

Once a company is public, sales of stock occur between the shareholders, and the company does not receive any of the proceeds from these sales.

### Merger & Acquisition

A company with publicly traded stock buys the stock of a private portfolio company. The end result is the holders of the portfolio company have their shares swapped with shares of the publicly traded company, hence creating a possible liquidity moment. M&A are probably the most common exit for venture capitalists.

### Reverse Merger

A reverse merger is a method of going public without doing an IPO. The process itself doesn't generate any cash, but the fact you have publicly traded stock may make your deal more palatable to investors – the deal is potentially more liquid. An operating nonpublic company merges into a non-operating public company (called a shell), and the result is a public company.

This kind of deal often has a stigma, so the entrepreneur should be careful when considering a reverse merger. Venture-backed companies rarely, if at all, utilize reverse mergers in order to become a public company.

Most of the companies that perform this maneuver do it in the hopes they subsequently will be able to attract investment (often sorely needed investment). Beyond the stigma associated with reverse mergers, most of these stocks are thinly traded. Let's say the average daily volume is 5,000 shares. If you hold 2 million shares of stock, you're not going to be able to sell many shares without causing a substantial drop in price.

## Secondary Offering

Once a company is public, it may be able to raise additional money by selling more stock to the public. A secondary offering is just like an IPO: The public buys shares of stock and the proceeds go to the issuing company.

## PIPE (private investment public entity)

In recent years many publicly traded companies have seen precipitous drops in their stock prices. Assuming the company's underlying fundamentals are still strong, these companies may be targets for PIPEs. This is a venture capital investment in a public company. Venture capitalists are warming to this type of investment because they have the possibility for faster liquidity – the portfolio company is already public.

### Extra Credit Reading: Dilution Rule

*If you're going to seek venture capital, you better understand what dilution means. It means you give up large chunks of equity--and control. Before you panic, remember: You are better off having part of something than all of nothing.*

# Lesson 6: Starting the Process

To understand how venture capital financing impacts companies, let's create a fictional company. Black Dog Enterprises, Inc. is a start up company in the burgeoning field of Labrador retriever cleaning technology. We will follow Black Dog's growth from an idea, to an early stage company, to a company that garners the interest and investment from venture capital firms, to a company that goes public.

We will track certain milestones and talk about the financing that is obtained to facilitate growth. We'll also look at the ownership issues and demonstrate what dilution means.

Before we begin, let's discuss two issues that seem to bedazzle many early stage entrepreneurs (and many graduates from top-flight MBA programs, too): 1) the different ways to capitalize a company, and 2) the oft-omitted issue of authorized shares and issued & outstanding shares.

## Ways to Capitalize a Company

Profits do not magically appear. Revenues do not come without associated costs. These costs include salaries, rent, insurance, utilities, capital investments, and all the other associated costs.

Where does this money come from? When you boil it down, companies have three main ways to obtain money: sell stock, issue debt, or use the company's earnings (also called bootstrapping). For those seeking extra credit, you can find reference to all of these on any company's balance sheet.

### Selling stock

When a company goes public, or raises a venture capital round, it is selling stock, or equity, in the company. Shades of gray exist – for reasons of liquidation preferences, venture deals are often in the form of debt that is convertible to equity – but essentially selling stock means you sell part of the company (or sell your personal stock), and this effectively is money the company never has to pay back. Selling equity means you give up ownership, and giving up ownership can have consequences.

### Borrowing money

This is called debt. It means you have to pay it back, usually plus interest. Holders of debt are higher on the liquidation food chain – holders of debt get their money before holders of common stock.

This is why venture capital deals are often convertible. The holders of debt will convert to equity only when it benefits them. If a company goes bankrupt, debt holders definitely are in a better position than equity holders. If a company goes public, equity holders probably are in a better position than debt holders.

### Retained earnings

Guess what? You can obtain the money you need to grow and/or sustain your business from the operations of your business. What a novel concept. If a company is profitable (or more precisely, cash flow positive), it will not have to seek funds to stay alive.

The problem with trying to grow a business using retained earnings is your cash flow is often not enough to cover heavy investments in personnel, equipment, and so forth. It is not impossible, of course. Another word for retained earnings is "bootstrapping."

## Authorized and Issued Shares

When a company is incorporated, the entrepreneur(s), lawyers, and other players decide how many shares of stock the company is authorized to issue. Authorized means the company can issue up to this amount, but not in excess of this amount. When a company sells stock, those shares are issued, and are considered outstanding.

If a company buys back some of its outstanding stock, that stock is called treasury stock. In keeping with the 101 nature of this document, we'll leave treasury stock discussions for the 300 level class.

Selling more shares than you are authorized to sell is called securities fraud, and it is against the law. The fact the company is private does not mean securities laws do not apply. A company must amend its articles of incorporation and by-laws if it wishes to increase the amount of authorized shares.

## Selling Stock

When selling stock, a company has two methods. First, current owners can sell all or part of their holdings. In this case, the proceeds from the sale go to the individuals who sold the stock, not the company.

Let's say we have a small manufacturing company, and the current owner, Frank, is in his sixties and wants to retire. The articles of incorporation say the company can legally issue up to 10,000 shares of stock. Currently, the company has 1,000 shares of stock issued and outstanding--all owned by Frank. Frank sells those 1,000 shares of stock to the new owner, Dean, for $1 million. Frank moves to Florida, and Dean owns the company

### *Pop Quiz*

*Let's say the entrepreneur and the venture capitalist agree that the value of the company, before investment, is $10 million. This is called the "pre money" valuation. Let's say $5 million is invested. What percentage of the company will the venture capitalists own?*

A.  25%
B.  33%
C.  50%
D.  67%

*The answer is B.  Since the pre-money valuation was $10 million, by virtue of putting $5 million into the company's checking account, the company would then have a post money value of $15 million. The new investors would therefore own 33% of the company's stock.*

The second option is for the company to issue new shares of stock in exchange for capital. In this example the funds go to the company, not the individual.

Let's say Dean hits some hard times and needs to bring in additional management/ownership, Sammy and Peter. Sammy and Peter agree to invest $500,000 into the business, which means the cash does not go to Dean. The money is used by the business for, say, paying down debt, upgrading equipment, and providing working capital.

Because the money flows to the company (instead of Dean) Dean does not sell any of his existing shares. Instead, the company issued 500 new shares to Sammy and Peter. The company now has 1,500 shares issued and outstanding. Dean owns 1,000 of them (or two thirds of the company), and Sammy and Peter collectively own 500 (or one third of the company).

Dean's holdings have been diluted; he owns less of the company (on a percentage basis), but unlike Frank, Dean hasn't seen his personal bank account increase in value.

Why would Dean agree to such a deal? Perhaps Dean realized if he didn't take the investment he would go out of business and lose everything. In addition to providing sorely needed capital, his new partners bring managerial and operational expertise, as well as a host of sales leads.

Without the investment, Dean would own 100% of nothing. With the investment Dean might own less of the company (on a percentage basis), but the company is stronger and better suited for long-term success. Dean is better off owning part of something than all of nothing.

## *Pop Quiz*

*A company has 5 million shares authorized, 1 million shares issued and outstanding. The CEO of the company owns 500,000 shares. How much of the company does he own?*

*A.  5%*
*B.  10%*
*C.  33%*
*D.  50%*

*The answer is D, 50%. Investors own a total of 1 million shares. Because the CEO owns one half of those shares, he owns 50% of the company. The amount of authorized shares is immaterial in calculating ownership percentages.*

Let's now return to Black Dog Enterprises as we talk about funding companies at the "idea" stage.

## Idea Stage

This is the "ah ha!" moment when someone, or a group of people, realize they have a business idea. Like a kid at Thanksgiving whose eyes are bigger than his stomach, entrepreneurs often think their idea's potential is bigger than it actually is.

In the case of Black Dog Enterprises, our entrepreneur (Mick), who will serve as CEO for the duration of our example, has a brainstorm and realizes the world desperately needs a better method for washing and cleaning Labrador Retrievers, dogs notorious for their oily coats.

In his free time he conducts some research and begins to formulate a plan. He simply needs intellectual property (IP), which is the process and device that washes dogs better. The IP will provide a sustainable competitive advantage for the company, mitigating investor risk. All Mick needs is the IP, and he is confident he can build a company.

Mick spent a number of years working in the dog washing technology business, attended a prestigious college (London School of Economics, I believe), and has many contacts in the industry.

By pure happenstance, Mick ran into Keith, an old elementary school buddy who, as it turns out, has been tinkering with a new method for dog washing. Keith calls it the "Dogs Are Dirty, Gonna Alleviate Drool" method, or DADGAD for short. Any resemblance to a guitar tuning used by the Rolling Stones is strictly coincidental.

Any dog that comes within 200 feet of a device embedded with DADGAD technology will be kept clean. While DADGAD works on all dogs, it is especially effective with Labrador retrievers. No more oily coats, no more sweeping dog hair, no more drool, no more noxious gases, no more dog breath, no more dander, no more wiping mud from your dog's paws.

People with allergies to dogs can now enjoy their company (as long as they are within 200 feet of a DADGAD device) without any ill effects. Keith has already filed and received two patents: one for the actual software, and the second on the process. It's truly a revolutionary technology.

Mick is obviously intrigued as Keith tells him what this technology can do. DADGAD can be embedded into a device as hardware, or, as Mick realizes, DADGAD can be employed as a software solution and delivered over the Internet. That's right; anyone with a computer and Internet can utilize DADGAD to maintain the cleanliness of their dog. I told you it was revolutionary.

"Revolutionary," Mick thinks to himself. "This is the technology I've been looking for."

Keith's original plan is to develop a box that contains the technology, and sell the box for $1,000 per unit. Mick proffers the idea that a software solution provides more scale with less associated costs (they won't have to produce and deliver boxes to retail stores). They should sell DADGAD as a subscription service.

What would people pay for this service? $20 a month is only $240 per year, and when you consider the costs of buying shampoo and other grooming products, and the time spent cleaning up after dogs, isn't $240 a year a bargain?

The software model also allows the company to create a recurring revenue stream while assuring users will have instant access to the latest updates and tweaks to the program.

Mick and Keith decide they will start a company to market Keith's DADGAD product. As they brainstorm business ideas they realize home users are not their only market. They can sell DADGAD to dog day care services, boarding facilities, animal hospitals, and city animal control units!

As they continue to brainstorm they realize dogs are not the only vertical. People with cats can use this product. People with rodents (as pets) can use this product. People with children can use this product.

Mick and Keith are convinced they can conquer the world.

They recruit a few other friends and industry contacts, Charlie, Bill, and Brian, and decide to start a company, and Black Dog Enterprises is organized as a corporation. The executives originally thought they should organize as a limited liability corporation (LLC), as it offers only one layer of tax. After their attorney pointed out the fact that VCs rarely invest in anything other than corporations, Black Dog is organized as a corporation.

Mick will be the CEO, Keith will be the president, and Charlie, Bill, and Brian all play other important roles. The ownership of the IP is transferred from Keith to the company (in exchange for stock). At this phase, 2 million shares are authorized, with 1.3 million issued and outstanding. Mick and Keith own an aggregate of 1 million shares of stock, or about 76.9% of the company.

The other three executives own an aggregate of 300,000 shares, or about 23.1%. All of this stock is "founders stock," and has no cost basis. The company is obviously pre-revenue, and for all intents and purposes, has not yet operated as a going concern.

Measuring milestones such as sales, earnings per share, net income, and so on, is moot. While the company likely has incurred some costs (legal fees), for the purposes of our example we are going to leave out that level of detail.

## Black Dog "Score Card"
### Idea Stage

| | | |
|---|---:|---:|
| pre money | $0 | 0% |
| investment | 0 | 0% |
| post money | $0 | 0% |
| Share price | $0 | 0% |

**Authorized Shares**

| | |
|---|---:|
| Common | 2,000,000 |

**Shares issued**

| | | |
|---|---:|---:|
| Founders | 1,000,000 | 77% |
| Other execs | 300,000 | 23% |
| Option plan | - | 0% |
| FF | - | 0% |
| Angel | - | 0% |
| VC - A | - | 0% |
| VC - B | - | 0% |
| VC - C | - | 0% |
| IPO | - | 0% |
| Total | 1,300,000 | 100% |

**Value of holdings**

| | |
|---|---:|
| Founders | $0 |
| Other execs | 0 |
| Option plan | 0 |
| FF | 0 |
| Angel | 0 |
| VC - A | 0 |
| VC - B | 0 |
| VC - C | 0 |
| IPO | 0 |
| Capitalization | $0 |

**Milestones (at time of funding)**

| | | |
|---|---|---:|
| Revenue | $ | - |
| Net Income | $ | - |
| Cash Flow | $ | - |
| EPS | | n/a |
| P/E | | n/a |
| Employees | | 5 |
| Rev/employee | | n/a |

## Friends and Family Investment

Black Dog's initial investment (beyond the time and small expenses associated with organizing the business) comes in the form of "friends and family." Black Dog does not have a marketable product, let alone actual sales.

Unless Mick and the boys are famous entrepreneurs (they're not), with a track record of successful start-ups (which they don't have), venture capitalist most likely will not be interested in the deal. Angel investors probably will not be interested, either.

Black Dog turns to people who will invest in the deal because they know, trust, and believe in Mick, Keith, Charlie, Bill and Brian: their friends and family. Black Dog raises a total of $100,000 from these people.

As they find out, the wooing is easier said than done. At first, Black Dog's team wants to raise enough money so they can all quit their jobs and focus full time of Black Dog. While they garner some interest from the friends and family, these would be investors balk at investing money simply to allow the team members to pay themselves a salary - especially because the salaries they want to pay themselves are all six figures.

The next point of contention is valuation. Keith believes the concept is the greatest thing since sliced bread, will revolutionize the world of dog washing, and as such, he believes they should be able to raise $1 million and only give up 1% of the company. Mick, being slightly more rational, introduces Keith to a new acronym, GYHOOYA.

"What's that?" asks a puzzled Keith, "a river in Ohio?"

"No, it means 'Get Your Head out Of Your Ass,'" retorts Mick. "No one is going to pay that kind of price for a company at our early stage of development. We do not have a product, we do not have sales or customers, and we're not even

100% sure at this time that our concept will work. What have you been smoking?"

"Price? I didn't say anything about price," responds Keith. "And I stopped smoking after the Toronto incident. Really, I have."

"You inferred price when you stated you wanted to sell 1% of our company for $1 million. That means our company would have a $100 million valuation. This poses a couple of problems. First, the company isn't worth $100 million at this time. While we hope it will be worth that much, and more, we have to deal with reality.

"Secondly, even if we induce our parents into buying stock at that high valuation, we will run into problems down the line because angels and VCs will not pay that kind of a premium. You have to remember, our 'greatest thing in the world' is their commodity. A VC sees 100 'greatest ideas in the world' every month.

"If we get the $100 million valuation from our early stage investors, it is a virtual certainty that they will have to take a "haircut" in future rounds. Taking a haircut means you're going to have to explain to Aunt Esther that the stock she thought was worth $1 per share is actually worth 5 cents per share. Are you looking forward to having that conversation? We have to avoid being myopic in our approach to raising money and building a business."

Black Dog eventually agrees to raise $100,000 by selling stock based on a pre money valuation of $200,000. The post money valuation, therefore, is $300,000. The investors are buying one third of the company ($100,000/$300,000). Since 1.3 million shares of stock are currently issued and outstanding, the company issues 650,000 new shares and sells those to the new investors for the agreement upon $100,000.

This raises the amount of stock issued to 1,950,000, of which 650,000 represents one third of the total issued and outstanding stock. Because Black Dog is now approaching its limit of 2 million authorized shares, the company will have to increase the amount of authorized shares before it can sell additional stock. Black Dog sold stock for about 15 cents per share (that is, $100,000/650,000).

Because new shares have been issued, the ownership positions of Mick, Keith, Charlie, Bill, and Brian have been diluted. Mick and Keith now collectively own 51.3% (compared to 76.9%), while the other three collectively own 15.4% (compared to 23.1%). On paper, all owners of Black Dog's stock have value, but because no market exists for Black Dog's stock, their holdings are extremely illiquid.

The company is still pre-revenue, and all five executives agree to continue working at their present jobs while they try to get Black Dog off the ground. All five will work on Black Dog in the evenings and weekends. They will also work on Black Dog during the day, as long as their current employers are not watching.

Black Dog is confident they will take no more than six months to build a company that will garner interest from venture capital firms. Black Dog's employees are looking forward to quitting their current jobs to focus exclusively on Black Dog.

## Black Dog "Score Card"
### Friends & Family Round

| | | |
|---|---:|---:|
| pre money | $200,000 | 67% |
| investment | 100,000 | 33% |
| post money | $300,000 | 100% |
| Share price | $0.15 | 0% |

| Authorized Shares | |
|---|---|
| Common | 2,000,000 |

| Shares issued | | |
|---|---:|---:|
| Founders | 1,000,000 | 51% |
| Other execs | 300,000 | 15% |
| Option plan | - | 0% |
| FF | 650,000 | 33% |
| Angel | - | 0% |
| VC - A | - | 0% |
| VC - B | - | 0% |
| VC - C | - | 0% |
| IPO | - | 0% |
| Total | 1,950,000 | 100% |

| Value of holdings | |
|---|---:|
| Founders | $153,846 |
| Other execs | 46,154 |
| Option plan | 0 |
| FF | 100,000 |
| Angel | 0 |
| VC - A | 0 |
| VC - B | 0 |
| VC - C | 0 |
| IPO | 0 |
| Capitalization | $300,000 |

| Milestones (at time of funding) | | |
|---|---|---:|
| Revenue | $ | - |
| Net Income | $ | - |
| Cash Flow | $ | - |
| EPS | | n/a |
| P/E | | n/a |
| Employees | | 5 |
| Rev/employee | | n/a |

# Angel Investment

After two long years, Black Dog finally offers an investment local angels will look at. The development of the product took far longer than expected, many unforeseen problems were encountered, everything took longer and cost more than was originally forecasted. The company still has many milestones to meet before it is a venture worthy company.

The main milestone Black Dog has obtained is they have a developed product, and they are ready to begin marketing, and if all goes according to plan, generating revenues. Black Dog's attorney has a client, Stu, who has invested in numerous early stage companies. Stu is known as an angel, a person who bridges the gap between friend and family financing and institutional financing (for example, venture capital).

While Stu does not run an investment company, he is far more methodical (and experienced) than Black Dog's friend and family investors. Black Dog has hired a couple of employees. Their low pay is compensated by the fact they are participating in Black Dog's stock option plan. The five founders of Black Dog are still not taking any pay from the company.

Stu is intrigued by the possibilities of Black Dog. He has already met a few of Black Dog's employees at local networking events, and has a friendly relationship with them. Stu simply likes Mick and Keith, thinks they are smart and dedicated, and believes they have a real chance of building Black Dog into a large company.

After a month of haggling, Stu and Black Dog agree to a $750,000 pre money valuation. Stu invests $350,000, which buys 956,667 shares of stock, or approximately 31.8% of the company.

As with the earlier round, Black Dog issues new shares (after the current investors agreed to increase the authorized shares to 5 million). Pursuit to the investment, the company sets up an incentive option program, with 100,000 options.

After Stu's investment, the company has a post money valuation of $1.1 million. While the first investors have been diluted, their holdings have increased in value. The $100,000 investment is now worth (on paper) $237,805.

Mick and Keith are concerned about the amount of the company they have to give up, but they take solace in the adage that they are better off owning part of something than all of nothing. While none of the five founders are currently taking a salary, they have all quit their day jobs, and have agreed to work full time at Black Dog. They have savings, and while they are not happy about having to dip into their nest eggs, they all feel the risk is worth it.

The $350,000 gives them cash to begin marketing the product. If they can start to generate revenues, they might be able to start taking small salaries...and go after a venture capital round.

# Black Dog "Score Card"
## Angel Round

| | | |
|---|---:|---:|
| pre money | $750,000 | 68% |
| investment | 350,000 | 32% |
| post money | $1,100,000 | 100% |
| Share price | $0.37 | 0% |

### Authorized Shares

| | |
|---|---:|
| Common | 5,000,000 |

### Shares issued

| | | |
|---|---:|---:|
| Founders | 1,000,000 | 33% |
| Other execs | 300,000 | 10% |
| Option plan | 100,000 | 3% |
| FF | 650,000 | 22% |
| Angel | 956,667 | 32% |
| VC - A | - | 0% |
| VC - B | - | 0% |
| VC - C | - | 0% |
| IPO | - | 0% |
| Total | 3,006,667 | 100% |

### Value of holdings

| | |
|---|---:|
| Founders | $365,854 |
| Other execs | 109,756 |
| Option plan | 36,585 |
| FF | 237,805 |
| Angel | 350,000 |
| VC - A | 0 |
| VC - B | 0 |
| VC - C | 0 |
| IPO | 0 |
| Capitalization | $1,100,000 |

### Milestones (at time of funding)

| | | |
|---|---|---:|
| Revenue | $ | - |
| Net Income | | $(120,000) |
| Cash Flow | | $(95,000) |
| EPS | | $(0) |
| P/E | | n/a |
| Employees | | 9 |
| Rev/employee | | n/a |

# Lesson 7: Do You Really Want Venture Capital?

If you are thinking about raising venture capital, repeat this mantra early and often:

*"Venture capital is probably the most difficult way for an entrepreneur to raise capital."*

## What Is Venture Worthiness?

Simply put, a company needs to obtain "critical mass" before VCs will take notice. Please repeat this mantra, "VCs invest in existing companies with existing sales; friends, family, and angels invest in start-ups."

The less risk your company mitigates, the less likely your company will be attractive to VCs. While no hard and fast rules exist as to how developed a company needs to be before it can obtain venture capital, here is a comprehensive list of areas of mitigation your company needs to offer VCs before they will be interested in your deal:

## Market Acceptance = Sales

One of the main risks your company needs to mitigate is market acceptance. Will the market buy your widget? You can compose lengthy tomes describing how you think the market will respond, but theoretic "what if" plans won't cut it. When it comes to market acceptance, only actual sales count.

## Existing Sales

In the post dotcom meltdown, post 9/11 world, VCs more than ever are demanding their potential portfolio companies have existing sales. Existing sales does not mean what an entrepreneur thinks his company will do in the next 6 months. Existing sales means how much money has flowed into your company during the past year.

VCs often look at trailing 12-month revenue stream as they decide whether or not to make an investment. Requirements vary from fund to fund, but many VCs will not even look at companies unless they have $1 million, $2 million (or more) in 12-month trailing revenue.

## Management Team

Are you an expert in the industry of your proposed business plan? What are your core competencies? Do you have an executive staff with a proven track record of 1) building business, 2) making gobs of money for other people, and 3) and doing what you propose to do?

The best way to phrase the management requirement is "been there, done that." Your company must have executives who have successful entrepreneurial experience, managed growing companies, and delivered results.

## Solve a Pressing Problem

The product must solve a pressing problem, and must not be a "solution looking for a problem." This is often one of the biggest stumbling blocks entrepreneurs face. Entrepreneurs run the risk of developing myopic vision, thinking their product/service is the greatest and most unique in the world.

This is where the entrepreneur most often needs the slap of reality: The better mousetrap theory is flawed. The world will NOT beat a path to your door if you are selling the "world's greatest mousetrap" to a target market that does not have a pestilence problem. Another way of looking at is this: would you buy the world's greatest headache cure if you do not have a headache?

Typical Venture Capital Target Industries

- Software: 199 (24%)
- Biotechnology: 81 (10%)

- Telecommunications: 75 (9%)
- Networking and equipment: 57 (7%)
- Medical devices: 73 (9%)
- Retailing/Distribution: 90 (11%)
- IT Services: 50 (6%)
- Semiconductors: 31 (4%)
- Computers and Peripherals: 27 (3%)
- Media and Entertainment: 28 (3%)
- Healthcare Service: 19 (2%)
- Industrial/Energy: 33 (4%)
- Financial Services: 14 (2%)
- Consumer Products/Services: 14 (2%)
- Electronics/Instrumentation: 10 (1%)
- Business Products/Services: 10 (1%)
- Other: 8 (1%)

*Total 819 (100%. Source: PricewaterhouseCoopers Q2 2002 MoneyTree Survey*

## Scalability

This refers to how easily your company can ramp up sales. As an example, consultancies typically are not attractive to VCs. If ten people generate $1 million in sales, the company likely will have to hire another 10 people to generate the second million. This is not scale! A better situation is to have a company were the first million in sales takes 10 people, hiring the 11th person allows the company to reach $2 million, and hiring the 12th person allows the company to reach $10 million in sales.

As with most things, scalability doesn't have a "secret sauce" or a right mix of elements. Investors will take in to consideration the following when trying to decide how well your business scales.

### Recurring revenue streams

Do you start each new month at zero, or does each sale add revenue that recurs each month? A business that starts each month at zero has a tougher time scaling. A steady stream of revenue (usually on a monthly or quarterly basis) is often better than a onetime only sale...unless that sale is a big-ticket item (in other words, the widget has a six-figure or higher price). AOL and other ISPs are examples of scale. The purchase price is not a one time only fee. Subscribers pay $20+ every month. AOL manages this part of its business by constantly looking to add subscribers. AOL does not have to go back and "resell" previous subscribers.

### Ease of sales

A week only contains 168 hours. How many of those hours are you able to take orders, 40, 80, 168? A company with 40-hour workweek may be more limited than a company that can take orders at 3 am on Sunday. Can you use technology to add more leverage to your sales operations? Clearly, this issue is mitigated if your company sells big-ticket items.

### Big ticket items

As mentioned above, selling big ticket items can be another way to scale a business. You might get to where you want to get a lot faster by selling at, say, $100,000 per item as opposed to $10 per item.

## Intellectual Property

Having intellectual property (IP) is often a desired way of mitigating investor risk. IP can increase the barriers of entry of your competitors. IP typically comes in the form of patents and trade secrets.

Setting up a business that washes dogs affords the investors no protection. Anyone could set up the same business. However, if your business utilized a unique technology that made it cheaper and faster to wash dogs and this was a technology that was owned solely by your company, this may represent a competitive advantage over potential competitors.

Having patents does not automatically assure the entrepreneur of a benefit. The product must solve a pressing need, but patents are also "breakable." Filing a patent means you disclose your "secret sauce." This makes it possible for competitors to look at your patent, and then design something similar, something that solves the same problem, but does not infringe on the patent.

A trade secret is simply when a company chooses to keep its "special sauce" private. The most famous trade secret is probably the formula to Coca-Cola, which has been used for over 100 years, far longer than any patent would have afforded protection.

Key takeaway: Patents are helpful, desired and useful, but they are not the "end all be all."

## The "Right" Industries

The typical industries that VCs invest in include software, biotech, telco, medical device, healthcare, and so on. These industries offer scale and high margins and reward proprietary technology.

If you are seeking venture capital for a real estate brokerage, a construction company, or your first retail store...good luck. Please see the table to the right for a recent example of venture capital target industries.

## Previous Investment

Unless your company has obtained a previous investment, a VC is unlikely to be the first investor in your deal. Quite simply, companies rarely obtain venture capital before obtaining "critical mass," and critical mass is difficult to obtain without some sort of previous investment.

Exceptions to this rule exist, of course. If a company has developed a product, obtained paying customers, and competes in an industry VCs find attractive, the fact the company has not yet sold stock will not be an obstacle for venture capital investment. Essentially, these companies have utilized bootstrapping as their financing tool, and one could argue this is a kind of investment.

## Realistic Sales Potential

The unwritten rule of thumb is VCs want to invest in companies that will grow to approximately $50 to $100 million in sales in a three to five year period. Business plans should obviously show this kind of growth.

If your plan shows your company will be generating $8 million in revenue in year 5, you do not have a venture worthy deal. Conversely, if your projections show the company zooming from zero to $2 billion in sales in 3 years, this will be viewed with a high degree of skepticism, and your plan will be filed in the trashcan.

Beyond showing the "right" level of sales growth, you must also explain the underlying assumptions that drive sales growth. VCs will spend a great deal of time pouring over every line of your financial projections. Make sure you have a logical and clear explanation for every factor that drives your revenues.

## Avoid the "Lump Of Clay" Syndrome

Do not expect a VC to put your company together. Do not present a mass of disparate ideas and expect the VC to extract the value. The entrepreneur must cleanly and clearly present the company, the opportunity, and the exit. In other words, have a concise and accurate business plan.

## Lingo

Understand the lingo of the venture capital world. When the discussion turns to Series A convertible preferred, warrants, EBITDA, and so on, you better know what they're talking about.

## Contact the Right Type of Investor

Do your homework and make sure the venture capital funds you target actually invest in your type of deal. A fund that invests in software and telecom deals probably will not be interested in a biotech company.

## Return

Understand the amount of risk taken and reward expected. VCs are looking for returns higher than those found in money market accounts, bond funds and stock funds. VCs usually look to earn 30% to 40% returns on their money. They expect this higher return because the risks they take are higher than the risk of putting money into a savings account.

## OK, I Don't Have A "Venture Worthy" Deal. What Can I Do?

It sounds flippant, but if you want to obtain venture capital financing, don't be a startup. Get beyond that phase. This is obviously easier said than done, but this is a basic premise the entrepreneur is not going to change. The questions then become: How do I get there? What are the steps needed to build a venture worthy company?

Instead of starting your capital search at venture capital firms, your best bet as an early stage entrepreneur is to bootstrap your business, utilize your network of friends and family, and eventually seek an angel investment.

# Lesson 8: Making the Approach

You're going to do it and no one can stop you. Here's how you can mitigate your risk and increase your chances you'll get a call back and/or conversation. Maybe even a meeting.

## The Approach – What Works

Many funds have on-line plan submission forms. Some funds are good at replying to inquiries, others are not, but this is often a good way of getting in the door. You're doing it their way.

Better than using an on-line submission form is having a referral to the fund. Short of having a referral, and if you don't want to utilize an on-line submission form, a good technique to make initial contact with a VCs is to make an phone call, then follow up with an e-mail. Simply sending a full plan "over the transom" is probably the weakest way to get the attention of a VC. It can work (sometimes), but the odds are against you.

Another consideration against the mass e-mail campaign is the fact that people receive so much junk e-mail today, getting a phone call/voice mail can often cut through the clutter.

Step 1: Do research and make sure you are calling the right person at the right firm. Venture capital funds usually have different people handle different types of deals. Most funds list their key people and their focus on their websites. If you cannot find this information, make a call to the general number and speak with a receptionist. Explain you are an entrepreneur, and you have a company in such-and-such industry and you're looking to talk with the person who handles these kinds of deal.

Step 2: Prepare a spiel, or elevator pitch. See the sample pitch below.

Step 3: Make the call (or get transferred to the correct person). You'll probably get voicemail, but be prepared to give your spiel to a live person. In both cases, pace is important. Don't talk slow, but don't rocket through your spiel, either. Take special care to slow down when you give your name and phone number. Many people seem to turbo-charge the speed at which they give their number, making it difficult to write down. If you have an unusual name, spell it (voicemail only). Speak clearly, deeply, with confidence and in a natural tone. Don't get cute, but don't sound rigid, either. You don't want to sound like you're reading from a script, and you don't want to sound like a hammy actor.

In the event you get a nibble, make sure you have all of the following documents at your ready access:

- 2 or 3 page executive summary
- Full business plan
- Historical financials (audited preferred, but probably not necessary). These should include income statement, balance sheet, and cash flow statement.
- 5 year projected financials, month-by-month for the first 2 years, and yearly for the final three. These should include income statement, balance sheet and cash flow statement.
- Detailed assumptions and staff roll out (to back up the projections)
- Client references
- Technical white papers (you might also want to prepare a "white paper" written for laypeople)

## Sample Pitch

*Calling Bob Mould, Principal at Husker Ventures:*

"Bob, this is Bill Snow with ABC Company, 312-555-5555. I was hoping to chat with you for a few moments about my company, to see if we might be a fit with your fund. We offer a software-based solution in the XYZ industry.

"We are largely subscription-based, with about 85% of our revenues recurring monthly. We launched the product 15 months ago, sales have increased each month since launch, and our 12-month trailing revenues are about $900K. Last month we did about $160K, which obviously is a $2 million run rate. We have a modest burn of about $20K per month, and we're forecasting to be cash flow positive within the next 6 to 12 months.

"Our technology is protected by 2 patents and one trade secret. We are looking to raise a $4 million series A. To-date, we've raised about $2 million, coming from some local angels and our founder. Our last round had a $4 million post money valuation.

"I'll be happy to answer any questions. If you prefer, I can e-mail you a 2-page summary. I also have the full plan, historical and projected financials, customer testimonials, and technical white papers. Tell me what you'd like to see at this time, and I'll be happy to get it to you.

"Again, this is Bill Snow, ABC Company, 312-555-5555."

In my pitch I clearly state who I am, the name of my company, and what we do. I accurately state our sales and investment history, mention our IP protection, and very clearly state that we are looking to raise money and I hope to speak to Bob to determine if we might fit his criteria.

I avoided being presumptuous in my approach. My spiel focuses on facts, not my opinion (which will only sound like a hyperbolic snake oil salesman). My approach is simple truth: I simply want to determine if this is a deal that Bob would like to look at.

Nowhere have I stated "this is the greatest thing in the world," nor have I falsely alluded to the fact that "time is running out, other investors are lining up, we about to close some HUGE deals, you better get in now while the gettin' is good."

Another good negotiating/presentation tip: When in doubt, go with facts instead of your opinion. Valuation, for example, is often a contentious issue between VC and entrepreneur. In the early phases of discussion, instead of proffering your opinion as to the company's valuation, simply stick with a fact: the valuation at the last round. Once you get down stream with an investor, you can hammer out the valuation issue.

## Follow Up

If you have the person's e-mail address you may want to jump-start the process by sending an e-mail with your contact information and perhaps the executive summary. This is a situation decision that the entrepreneur needs to make based on his gut feel.

You will be surprised at how often you will receive a returned call or e-mail if your company actually meets the VC's criteria. This technique is not 100% effective (none are), and other ways to make initial contact with a VC exist, but this has worked for me.

## Be Prepared For Callbacks

Memorize your deal facts, know whom you've contacted, and be prepared to talk about your deal at a moment's notice. These are some of the questions you should expect:

- What is the value proposition for the investor?
- What makes your deal different?
- Who are your competitors and why are you better? Why are you going to win?
- What is your revenue model and what is your current revenue run rate?
- What events will positively or negatively impact revenue?
- How does the current business/political environment affect your business? Do you benefit, suffer, or is the impact negligible, and why?
- What is the average ROI for your customers?

- How do your customers measure the results of your product?
- What is your sales cycle? What is the length of time from identifying customers to receiving a signed contact?
- What is the average cost per unit?
- Where does this funding round get you? Breakeven, cash flow positive, and so on?
- What were your sales last year?
- What are this year's sales?
- How much money has been invested?
- Who are your investors?
- What is your burn rate?

If you cannot provide direct and simple answers (that is, three sentences or less) to each of these simple questions, you still have some homework to do. Beyond rote memorization, you need make sure your answers sound natural, not "canned."

## The Approach – What Doesn't Work

Now that we have examined what works, let's take a look at some of the boneheaded things entrepreneurs do in trying to contact VCs.

- Mass e-mailing your plan to hundreds of venture capital firms. This gaffe is multiplied if you send the plans without considering if the fund(s) actually invest in your type of company. This gaffe is multiplied further if your business plan is a monolithic tome better suited to doorstop duty. The mass e-mailing technique is usually seen as an act of desperation or an act of stupidity. Pick your poison, neither is a good thing.
- A request for the reader to sign a non-disclosure agreement (NDA). VCs generally do not sign NDAs.
- Plans lacking sales figures. If a deal is "pre-revenue," most VCs will pass. Such deals would more likely benefit from angel investors.
- Plans that show unrealistic sales growth.
- Featuring a management team that lacks industry experience.

- Featuring a management team that has not previously built and/or run substantial businesses or business units. (Running a $3 million tuckpointing business usually will not count.)
- Trying to raise venture capital for products that are difficult to sell and difficult to scale.

# Lesson 9: Business Plan Basics

Many entrepreneurs do not think they have to write a business plan. In a similar vein, a good friend of mine, while seeking a job years ago, refused to create a resume, saying, "My resume is my mouth." While this seat-of-the-pants approach often provides a desirable breathless urgency about your deal (or career), more often than not the entrepreneur is better off writing a plan, just as a job seeker is better off creating a resume.

That said, if you can raise money without writing a plan, then do so! But the fact is most VCs will want to see something on paper. They will want something tangible, something they can forward to a colleague. The business plan is often a good academic exercise for the entrepreneur, "forcing" him to mentally work out certain issues.

When writing a plan, the main thing to remember is investors will not "dig" for answers when reviewing it. If the opportunity fails to grab the reader's attention, the cause is likely to be one of two reasons: 1) the opportunity is not venture worthy or 2) the entrepreneur has not concisely and simply explained the opportunity. Plans need to be simple, easy to read, powerful, and to the point. Complexity for complexity's sake will not impress.

While your plan (and underlying opportunity) is graded on a curve, the curve is extremely steep. If your opportunity is the best of a bad bunch, you're not getting funded. The fact that VCs have recently returned money to their limited partners (instead of making investments) testifies to this fact.

## Don't Recreate History

Do not waste time showing off your encyclopedic knowledge of the history of technology and communication. Investors have heard about this thing called "the Internet." They know the history of communication. They know all about the telephone, telegraph, fax machine, electricity, and stirrup. Tell them what they don't know.

## Venture Capitalists Don't Know Anything About YOUR Deal!

Focus on that fact. Your plan needs to educate the reader as to the how, what, where, why, and when of your company. This is basic college freshman year term paper stuff. On the following page I've listed some of the basic questions your plan needs to answer.

### Basic Questions Your Plan Needs To Answer

- What do you sell?
- How much have you sold?
- Whom do you sell to?
- How do you sell?
- Where do you sell it?
- How do you price it?
- What market pain do you solve?
- What is the stage of your product development?
- What is the compelling reason the market will buy your widget?
- What is your revenue model?
- How do you make money?
- Why are you going to win?
- Who are your competitors and how are you different from them?
- What are your milestones?

If the reader cannot divine the answers to these questions from a cursory look at your plan, the reader probably will not get these answers from a deeper study of your plan because your plan will not receive a deeper study. You must immediately and explicitly address each of these questions. Failure to do so will likely send your plan to the trash pile.

If, for some reason, you decide to disregard this advice, at least get your facts right. During autumn 2001, as we were suffering through the stock market swoon and the effects of 9/11, I reviewed a plan where the author, in his executive summary, talked about the "the booming stock market" and how "corporate earnings are at record highs." At the time NASDAQ was 60% percent below its peak and a long string of companies were announcing enormous losses.

An article I saved for a period of time, "NASDAQ Companies' Losses Erase 5 Years of Profits," (Wall Street Journal, 8/16/01) was on my desk at the time I reviewed the plan. The entrepreneur effectively demonstrated his considerable lack of industry knowledge -- which obviously didn't bode well for his opportunity.

## Keep It Simple

Beowulf is a long, complicated 1200-year-old Anglo-Saxon poem. Your business plan should not be comparable to Beowulf. VCs will not pour over every line, looking for hidden meaning and nuance. This is not a freshman English class dissecting a 10th century Anglo-Saxon poem. The reader will not spend three hours, let alone three days, scouring your plan. You must make it compelling and easy to read.

## Pithy

Your plan should not exceed 25 pages of narration and 10 pages of historical and projected financials. For ease of transmission, keep the plan to less than 1 MB. Make sure all of your documents are in electronic format. This is the preferred method of dissemination.

The narration should include management bios, and the financials (historical and projected) should include "full set" (income statement, balance sheet, and cash flow statement information) with REALISTIC projections for the next three to five years. As back-up information, have white papers, sales funnels, and client references available upon request.

In your business plan and elevator pitch, do not recap the evolution of the Internet and do not restate the current economic situation. Investors know these things. You must grab the investor's attention within 20 seconds. You must immediately state your value proposition and how your investor will realistically make a ton of money.

If you cannot make a compelling case for your deal in 25 pages of narration, bloating it up to 100 pages won't make a difference. VCs do not have time to read long plans.

## Are Your Historical Financials Relevant?

Many entrepreneurs submit plans that show their companies have existing sales. Good, right? Not if the company's past sales represent technologies that are not part of the future plans and not if the future technologies have not yet been fully developed.

In this case, the company will be considered "pre-revenue," because no revenue has been derived from the technology of the future. A better option for entrepreneurs in this position might be to contact an attorney, incorporate a new company and finance it with the proceeds from selling the old company or old technology.

## Know Your Competition

Everyone has competition. Even though you may not be up against a pure play competitor, you are competing with someone in the marketplace either inadvertently or head-on. Don't insult a VC by telling him you face no competition. Saying you face zero competition simply means you haven't done your homework.

Touting the fact you think you face zero competition is merely touting the fact you are either stupid or unprepared – or both.

## Be Realistic

A plan that shows a company going from zero to $2 billion in sales in only five years -- with only $3 million of paid-in capital -- is extremely unlikely. Do your homework and research other companies in your space. What kind of sales growth did they achieve? How much investment was required to generate those sales?

Better yet, go to http://finance.yahoo.com/ and take a look at the balance sheets of large public companies. You will not find billion dollar companies with miniscule amounts of equity on their balance sheets.

## The "First Step" Syndrome

Is your plan reasonable, or does it depend on a series of improbable events that all need to occur in order for the business to succeed? Many plans are faulty from the start because they project impossible levels of growth. This is called the "first step."

If you have a company that is generating, say, $80,000 per month, receiving an investment of $5 million will not suddenly increase your monthly sales total to $2 million. Many steps exist before your company will see a sizable increase in revenues.

This problem occurs when projected sales figures look good but are not rooted in sound assumptions. For example, hiring 30 people tomorrow and expecting them to immediately operate at 100% capacity pretty much is an impossibility.

Even if you can reasonably expect each new employee to produce a certain amount of revenue, can you really staff up and support all those people within the time constraints of your plan? Hiring and training people takes time. Buying and installing software takes time. Hooking up phones and networks takes time. Even if you have the money to hire and buy to your heart's content, do you have enough time to adequately set every thing up?

## What Is Your Company's True Revenue Ceiling?

Very few companies have the product horsepower to be $100 million concerns, let alone $1 billion companies. Most companies have gross revenues of less than $5 million per year. What is the real revenue potential for your company? Here's a clue: If your sales have remained flat for a couple of years, chances are that additional investment will not yield higher sales. All companies have a revenue ceiling.

## The Employee Downward Spiral

Odds are your President, CEO and other founders will be your best sales people. They founded it, they understand it, they are betting their own money, and they live, sleep, and breath the company.

The larger a company becomes and the more people it employs, the less new employees will exhibit the same level of buy in. To assume employee #200 will be able to execute a sales plan at the same level and intensity of employee #10 is often foolhardy, and more than likely, fatal. The further from your CEO, the lower the performance. Do not assume every employee will perform at a CEO level.

## Avoid the Current Year Revenue Trap

This is one of those areas that often inadvertently trip up entrepreneurs. In the rush to self promote, many entrepreneurs blur the line between actual results and hoped-for results. For example: A company that hasn't booked dollar one in revenue will say, on December 30th, "current year sales are $2 million." They are obviously hoping 100% of their revenue will occur on the last day of the year. What kind of odds would you put on this?

A better way to state the current year's sales is to use 12-month trailing revenue and use the current run rate.

# Lesson 10: Financials

Financials are often one of the biggest shortcomings of early stage entrepreneurs' business plans. The reasons are myriad: limited financial/accounting background, dislike of finance/accounting, focus on everything but finance/accounting, and so on. A common complaint seems to be:

*"What's the point? The actual result will be completely different than any projection. We can spend a lot of time creating and refining our model, but not one number will occur as our projections show."*

This, of course, is completely true. The likelihood is small that any single number in a set of projected financials will occur in real life. What is important, and why this exercise is so necessary, is that the entrepreneur needs to demonstrate complete understanding of his company's operations. What are the ratios, what factors affect what numbers, what happens to output A if input B is increased 10%?

Your investors need to know you have a full and complete grasp of your industry, your product, and your sales process. Entrepreneurs at all levels need to understand financial statements, how to read them, and how to create ACCURATE projections.

A business plan should contain two sets of financials, historical and projected, and they should be presented as a "full set," that is, income statement, balance sheet and cash flow statement.

Beyond the mere inclusion of these documents, entrepreneurs should understand how each of these documents work. I recall talking to an early stage entrepreneur who didn't know the difference between operating cash flow and financing cash flow. He actually considered raising equity (from selling stock) as a function that shows up on the income statement as revenue!

## Historical Financials

This is the first part of the financials section, and the easy part. Historical financials are simply a report on your company's past. These are the numbers that have been "embalmed" by your accountant: they are dead and buried and will not change.

## Projected Financials

Probably one of the most vexing challenges facing entrepreneurs is the creation of financial projections. How fast should the company grow? What do VCs want to see? What is realistic? How important are these darned projections?

Let's face facts, most financial projections follow roughly the same revenue trajectory on the income statement: a couple hundred thousand in year one, $5-8 million year two, $15-25 million year three, $40-50 million year four, $75-100 million year five.

The issue isn't what the top line numbers say. To be frank, those numbers are pulled from thin air. The real issue is the support mechanism offered to support the top line numbers. This support mechanism is the assumptions page.

## Assumptions

This is the hidden financial statement, the one that isn't discussed in college accounting courses. Yet, it may be the most important statement an entrepreneur will ever create. The friendly confines of the assumptions page contain the financial model's secret sauce.

The key to good assumptions is the differentiation between "top-down" and "ground-up." Top-down means inventing good looking top line revenue figures, then plugging in seemingly appropriate (and smaller) numbers for all the subsequent line items, yielded a very handsome profit in the later years of the plan.

The problem with this approach is that the numbers are massaged to look "good," but they really aren't based on reality. For example, what if the plan is still showing losses when you think it should be profitable? How about cutting salary expense until you show a suitable profit?

The risk you run is that by making the numbers look "good," you might have an unworkable model. You might show a profit, but how reasonable are all the line item expenses? Employing this method might result in a plan with $20 million in revenue and only $100,000 in total salary expense.

The way to build assumptions is from the "ground up," that is, starting with estimating everything on the smallest basis possible, then adding every upwards to come up with your top line revenue number.

The place to employ the top-down method is double-checking to make sure you projections are rooted in reality. Are you in line with your competitors, or do you show stunning differences?

If you are projecting average sales per employee twice the rate of your industry, what compelling reason do you offer? Do you offer a technique or technology that supports your assumption, and if so, what is that stunning and sustainable competitive advantage? Or are you guilty of not doing your homework?

Here are some tips and things to think about as you construct your assumptions.

## Revenue Drivers

The initial step in creating your assumptions and financial projections is to determine what drives revenue. Sales will not magically appear simply because you put them down on your spreadsheet. Does your company rely on an outside sales force? If so, how many phone calls and site visits can you realistically expect your employees to handle?

If your top line revenue estimations are dependent upon your sales people working 30 hours a day, making 60 calls per hour (with each call lasting 10 minutes), and visiting 25 clients per day (each visiting lasting one hour), these are obviously impossible expectations.

Every business has different drivers, so providing a concrete example that will work for every business is impossible. Regardless of the business, you should ask yourself some standard questions:

- How do you generate revenue? Outside sales, Internet, commissions?
- How many sales people do you need to reach a given sales level?
- What is your sales cycle? How long does it take to close a deal?

## Cost of Goods Sold

What are the costs of the raw material directly associated with generating a given amount of revenue? This is your cost of goods sold (COGS). Subtracting the COGS from revenue yields the gross margin. Some companies, such as manufacturing concerns, have clear COGS lines. Raw materials such steel, rubber, wood, plastic, computer chips, processors, and so forth, are easy to tally. Other industries, such as software, the direct COGS line is difficult to figure. Check with your accountant if you're not sure what to include in your COGS.

## Operational Expenses

As we learned in Accounting 101 in college, operational expenses are typically expressed as either fixed or variable expenses. For the purpose of building a financial model, most of the expenses are going to be variable, although it may make sense to "hardwire" some of the expenses (a marketing program, for example).

Most of these expenses can be based on a per employee rate or as a percentage of sales. Here's a quick primer of some of the main operational expenses, and how you should estimate them:

- Salary expense - create a separate staff roll out
- Payroll expense - percentage of salary expense
- Marketing & advertising - percentage of revenue, although you may want to "hardwire" this amount if you plan to execute a detailed plan. You should include that plan as an additional worksheet.
- Meals and entertainment - per employee basis
- Sales promotion - percentage of sales
- Travel - per employee basis
- Web site - percentage of sales, although this may be a "hardwired" number
- Sales commissions - percentage of sales
- Insurance (health, dental, property & liability, workers comp, etc) – per employee basis
- Professional fees (legal, accounting) – percentage of sales
- Payroll service – per employee basis
- Dues & subscriptions – percentage of sales
- Rent – per employee basis
- Equipment rental – per employee basis
- Office supplies – per employee basis
- Postage – per employee basis
- Utilities (phone, electricity, Internet) – per employee basis
- Vehicle expense – per employee basis

A key thing to remember is many of these expenses will grow with revenue (or employees) on a one for one basis. A 100% increase in sales will necessitate a 100% increase in the particular line item. Most of these expenses will see economies of scale as the company grows. For example, professional fees may be 20% of sales in year 1, but you definitely do not want to see that kind of percentage in year 5 when the projections show a $100 million company.

## Salary Expense

Hey! Lookie here! Many of the expenses of a business are tied to the number of employees. Having a separate worksheet that calculates the number of employees needed for a given revenue level is critical.

The other reason is because salary expense probably will be the biggest expense of your company. Frankly, all the other expense items are small potatoes.

What employees offer scale? Which ones need to be hired on a one for one basis with increases in sales? How quickly can you hire and train new employees.

- Sales People – how many sales people will you need to acquire certain levels of revenue. How much do you expect each person to produce?
- Marketing people – how many marketing people do you need to support the efforts of sales?
- Operations – how many people do you need to fulfill orders and maintain high levels of customer service?
- IT and technical people – do you only need a few people to maintain your network, or does your sales and implementation process involve technical people? Do you need to set up "teams" to sell and maintain your product: three sales people supported by one technical expert, perhaps?
- Accounting and finance people – general rule, the bigger you get the fewer (on percentage terms) accountants you'll need.
- Executives – this should be hardwired. You'll only need one CEO, one CFO, one COO and one VP of Sales. Depending on the particularities your business you may need a few other executives.
- Administrative assistants – how many support people will you need?

- Research & development – does your company need people to develop the next iteration of your product?

## Income Statement, Balance Sheet, Cash Flow Statement

Most projections include an income statement. Fewer offer a balance sheet, and fewer still offer a cash flow statement. Your plan should include all three, and of these three, the cash flow statement is the most important.

Since this is a 101 course, we're not going to delve into the minutia of accounting, but the cash flow statement is the document that ties together the income statement and balance sheet and follows the flow of money in three key areas:

- Financing - money obtained (or used) from selling (or buying) stock or debt.
- Investing - money used (or obtained) from buying (or selling) equipment, facilities, and so on.
- Operations – money obtained (or lost) from doing what your company is really supposed to be doing – selling a good or service.

Your financial statements should project 5 years into the future. The first 2 years should be on a month-by-month basis, while the final three can be annual.

## Focus On EBITDA, Not Taxable Income

Who wants to pay to taxes? A truer measure of your company's operating performance is its earnings before interest, taxes, depreciation and amortization, or EBITDA. What the EBITDA figure does is strip away all the ancillary financial factors and shows an earnings number based on the internal performance of your company.

In other words, are you doing what you're supposed to do? Are you actually selling the product your investors think you're supposed to be selling?

# Lesson 11: Raising Venture Capital Rounds

Now that we've covered some of the basics, let's return to Black Dog and see how they fare with the VCs.

## Venture Investment – Series A

One year after Stu's angel investment, Black Dog is showing strong signs of life. The company generated $700,000 in revenue for the trailing 12-month period, and all five of the founders were able to start taking small salaries. The company is still losing money, but they forecast given their sales growth, they should be a cash flow positive within 6 to 12 months.

Beyond the need for cash to cover their current burn rate, they realize they need money to hire some new employees and start a full force marketing campaign. Even after they become profitable, the profits will not be large enough to cover these costs.

Mick and Keith realize with their sales track record, the scalability of sales, the demand for the service, and patent protection, they might have a venture worthy deal.

The one area Black Dog is weak in is executive management. While all five are talented and intelligent, they don't have anyone who they would consider as "been there, done that."

After a long conversation, Mick and Keith realize Brian isn't the manager they hoped he would be. Brian played a crucial role in the early years, but recently he seems out of his element, and Mick and Keith decide to replace Brian. After a false start with another executive (who is fired, too), Ron, a savvy old pro is brought on board, and Black Dog's core team is finally set.

Mick and Keith put together a business plan and begin to contact VCs known to invest in the dog-washing technology vertical. Searching for venture capital takes six months, and after Iggy Ventures is identified, the deal takes another 3 months to complete. Mick and Keith are surprised it took almost a full year to complete the investment.

At the end of the day, Iggy Ventures offers to invest $2 million with a pre money valuation of $3 million, meaning they are buying 40% of the company. The option plan is increased to 250,000 options, further diluting Black Dog's original backers. The authorized shares are increased to 5 million, and 2,104,444 shares are issued in exchange for the $2 million investment.

When the Series A closes, Mick and Keith's aggregate ownership is down to a 19%, while the other executives hold a total of 5.7% of the company's outstanding stock. The family members, who provided the first investment and once owned 33% of the company, now hold 12.4%. Stu, the angel, now owns 18.2% of the company, down from his initial 31.8% position.

While Mick and Keith are concerned about the steep price they will pay for the round, they remind themselves they have created value from nothing. Beyond providing sorely needed cash, Iggy Ventures brings industry expertise and sales contacts.

All parties agree having part of something is better than having all of nothing. Iggy Ventures' investment will hopefully bring everyone a little closer to owning a piece of a big pie.

# Black Dog "Score Card"

## VC - A Series

| | | |
|---|---|---|
| pre money | $3,000,000 | 60% |
| investment | 2,000,000 | 40% |
| post money | $5,000,000 | 100% |
| Share price | $0.95 | 0% |

### Authorized Shares

| | |
|---|---|
| Common | 10,000,000 |

### Shares issued

| | | |
|---|---|---|
| Founders | 1,000,000 | 19% |
| Other execs | 300,000 | 6% |
| Option plan | 250,000 | 5% |
| FF | 650,000 | 12% |
| Angel | 956,667 | 18% |
| VC - A | 2,104,444 | 40% |
| VC - B | - | 0% |
| VC - C | - | 0% |
| IPO | - | 0% |
| Total | 5,261,111 | 100% |

### Value of holdings

| | |
|---|---|
| Founders | $950,370 |
| Other execs | 285,111 |
| Option plan | 237,592 |
| FF | 617,740 |
| Angel | 909,187 |
| VC - A | 2,000,000 |
| VC - B | 0 |
| VC - C | 0 |
| IPO | 0 |
| Capitalization | $5,000,000 |

### Milestones (at time of funding)

| | |
|---|---|
| Revenue | $700,000 |
| Net Income | $(400,000) |
| Cash Flow | $(300,000) |
| EPS | $(0) |
| P/E | n/a |
| Employees | 18 |
| Rev/employee | $38,889 |

## Venture Investment – Series B

One year after Iggy Ventures' investment, Black Dog's 12-month trailing revenue is $2 million, and the company is cash flow positive. Black Dog now employees 35 people.

While they are happy with the growth and the cash flow positive status, Black Dog's executives realize they will need more cash if they plan to rapidly grow the business. The company is currently generating about $150,000 per year of free cash flow.

Black Dog realizes it can continue to grow without new investment, but this rate of growth will be very slow. Perhaps in 5 years they'll generate $10 million in revenue, far below the expectations of Black Dog's investors.

To expedite growth, Mick and Keith create a new business plan. The plan calls for a national advertising and branding campaign, investment in capital equipment, more research and development, and, of course, more employees.

The $10,000 or so the company is generating each month as free cash flow is nowhere near what the company needs to fund its growth plan. Black Dog decides to go back to the venture capital world to obtain expansion capital.

Because more risks have been mitigated, Black Dog's Series B investment path is much shorter than the Series A. The fact Black Dog already has venture investment makes the path easier, too. Iggy Ventures helps introduce Black Dog to some new investors, funds that invest in later stage deals.

After 4 months of negotiation, the new fund agrees to invest $4 million in Black Dog at a $7 million pre million money valuation. The post money valuation is $11 million, and the new investors own 36.4% of Black Dog. The option plan is increased to 500,000 shares, further diluting the current owners.

3,149,206 new shares are issued and sold in exchange for the $4 million investment. Approximately 8.6 million shares of Black Dog are issued and outstanding, still under the authorized limit of 10 million.

## Black Dog "Score Card"
### VC - B Series

| | | |
|---|---:|---:|
| pre money | $7,000,000 | 64% |
| investment | 4,000,000 | 36% |
| post money | $11,000,000 | 100% |
| Share price | $1.27 | 0% |

| Authorized Shares | |
|---|---|
| Common | 10,000,000 |

| Shares issued | | |
|---|---:|---:|
| Founders | 1,000,000 | 12% |
| Other execs | 300,000 | 3% |
| Option plan | 500,000 | 6% |
| FF | 650,000 | 8% |
| Angel | 956,667 | 11% |
| VC - A | 2,104,444 | 24% |
| VC - B | 3,149,206 | 36% |
| VC - C | - | 0% |
| IPO | - | 0% |
| Total | 8,660,317 | 100% |

| Value of holdings | |
|---|---:|
| Founders | $1,270,161 |
| Other execs | 381,048 |
| Option plan | 635,081 |
| FF | 825,605 |
| Angel | 1,215,121 |
| VC - A | 2,672,984 |
| VC - B | 4,000,000 |
| VC - C | 0 |
| IPO | 0 |
| Capitalization | $11,000,000 |

| Milestones (at time of funding) | |
|---|---:|
| Revenue | $2,000,000 |
| Net Income | $(50,000) |
| Cash Flow | $150,000 |
| EPS | $(0) |
| P/E | n/a |
| Employees | 35 |
| Rev/employee | $57,143 |

# Venture Investment – Series C

One year after the Series B, Mick and Keith's growth plan is paying dividends. The new cash allowed the company to hire 40 new people, launch a very successful advertising campaign, and invest in R&D. Sales hit $15 million, and the company's free cash flow is $750,000.

Even though the company is profitable, it still has cash needs beyond its cash flow. For similar reasons, Black Dog decides to do a 3rd round of venture financing. Black Dog looks as if it has a very good chance of doing an IPO in a few years, and this helps to further mitigate investor risk and increase valuation

Once approved by the board of directors, the authorized shares are increased to 20 million, and with the assistance of Black Dog's current investors, and third venture capital firm, specializing in "mezzanine" financing is brought in.

This round raises $5 million at a $15 million pre money valuation. 2,970,106 shares of stock are issued and exchange for the $5 million investment. The new investors hold 25% of the company's issued and outstanding stock. The stock option plan is increased to 750,000 shares.

As with every other round of financing during Black Dog's growth, past investors have been diluted. Mick and Keith now own an aggregate of 8.4%, the other executives own 2.5%, friends and family own 5.5%, and the angel 8.1%. The holders of series A stock hold 17.7% and the holders of series B stock hold 26.5%

With $12 million in annual sales, all associated with Black Dog figure a liquidity moment isn't far away.

# Black Dog "Score Card"
## VC - C Series

| | | |
|---|---:|---:|
| pre money | $15,000,000 | 75% |
| investment | 5,000,000 | 25% |
| post money | $20,000,000 | 100% |
| Share price | $1.68 | 0% |

### Authorized Shares
| | |
|---|---:|
| Common | 20,000,000 |

### Shares issued
| | | |
|---|---:|---:|
| Founders | 1,000,000 | 8% |
| Other execs | 300,000 | 3% |
| Option plan | 750,000 | 6% |
| FF | 650,000 | 5% |
| Angel | 956,667 | 8% |
| VC - A | 2,104,444 | 18% |
| VC - B | 3,149,206 | 27% |
| VC - C | 2,970,106 | 25% |
| IPO | - | 0% |
| Total | 11,880,423 | 100% |

### Value of holdings
| | |
|---|---:|
| Founders | $1,683,442 |
| Other execs | 505,033 |
| Option plan | 1,262,581 |
| FF | 1,094,237 |
| Angel | 1,610,493 |
| VC - A | 3,542,710 |
| VC - B | 5,301,505 |
| VC - C | 5,000,000 |
| IPO | 0 |
| Capitalization | $20,000,000 |

### Milestones (at time of funding)
| | |
|---|---:|
| Revenue | $12,000,000 |
| Net Income | $500,000 |
| Cash Flow | $750,000 |
| EPS | $0 |
| P/E | 40 |
| Employees | 75 |
| Rev/employee | $160,000 |

# Lesson 12: The Exit

One year after receiving their series C investment, and with revenues hitting $32 million for the year, Black Dog successfully goes public, raising $50 million by selling a little over 20% of the company's stock.

This gives the company a market capitalization of $240 million. Black Dog pays their investment bankers an 8% fee for the arranging the IPO, meaning the net proceeds to the company are $46 million.

The stock begins the day trading at $14.92 a share. At this price, here's how all of the participants have fared:

Mick and Keith's holdings are worth just under $15 million on the day of the IPO. Because they each own the same amount of stock, they're each worth a cool seven and half million dollars.

The other executives in the company have collective holdings worth about $4.4 million.

The company option plan has a value of almost $24 million. In addition to company's 150 employees, Mick, Keith, and the other executives all have options, too.

The friends and family, who invested the original $100,000 7 years ago, are now worth $9.7 million. Stu, the angel who invested $350,000 six years ago, now owns over $14 million worth of Black Dog stock.

Iggy Ventures, the firm that invested $2 million in the series A four years ago, owns over $31 million of Black Dog Stock. The firm that invested $4 million in the series B round three years ago owns $47 million of Black Dog stock.

The series C investors, who put in $5 million a year ago, now own $44 million worth of Black Dog. Plenty of people associated with Black Dog have big smiles.

The venture capital firms, per their operating agreements, begin to sell their holdings almost immediately. Fearful of placing too much sell pressure on the stock, and thereby lowering the price, the VCs sell their holdings over a period of 12 months. The other investors all refrain from selling.

## Black Dog "Score Card"

### IPO

| | | |
|---|---:|---:|
| pre money | $190,000,000 | 79% |
| investment | 50,000,000 | 21% |
| post money | $240,000,000 | 100% |
| Share price | $14.92 | 0% |

| Authorized Shares | | |
|---|---:|---|
| Common | 100,000,000 | |

| Shares issued | | |
|---|---:|---:|
| Founders | 1,000,000 | 6% |
| Other execs | 300,000 | 2% |
| Option plan | 1,600,000 | 10% |
| FF | 650,000 | 4% |
| Angel | 956,667 | 6% |
| VC - A | 2,104,444 | 13% |
| VC - B | 3,149,206 | 20% |
| VC - C | 2,970,106 | 18% |
| IPO | 3,350,111 | 21% |
| Total | 16,080,535 | 100% |

| Value of holdings | |
|---|---:|
| Founders | $14,924,877 |
| Other execs | 4,477,463 |
| Option plan | 23,879,803 |
| FF | 9,701,170 |
| Angel | 14,278,132 |
| VC - A | 31,408,574 |
| VC - B | 47,001,517 |
| VC - C | 44,328,464 |
| IPO | 50,000,000 |
| Capitalization | $240,000,000 |

| Milestones (at time of funding) | |
|---|---:|
| Revenue | $32,000,000 |
| Net Income | $1,800,000 |
| Cash Flow | $2,400,000 |
| EPS | $0 |
| P/E | 133 |
| Employees | 150 |
| Rev/employee | $213,333 |

One year post IPO, Black Dog's stock has increased from $15 to $35 per share. This has increased the company's market cap to $560 million. Mick and Keith are now worth $35 million total, or $17.5 million each.

The other executives now hold a total of $10 million of Black Dog. The friends and family are worth almost $23 million, while Stu's holdings are worth over $33 million. The public market investors, who invested $50 million in Black Dog, now have shares worth over $117 million.

Five years post IPO, Black Dog's stock is traded at $135 per share, giving Mick and Keith a total value of $135 million, or $67.5 million each. The other executives' holdings now exceed $40 million.

The friends and family value is approaching $90 million, and Stu, holding almost $130 million worth of stock, spends his days sailing his boat in the Caribbean Sea.

The venture capital funds, had they held on to their shares, would collectively own over $1.2 billion of Black Dog.

## Black Dog "Score Card"

| | IPO +1 yr | | IPO +5 yrs | |
|---|---|---|---|---|
| pre money | $0 | | $0 | |
| investment | 0 | | 0 | |
| post money | $0 | | $0 | |
| Share price | $35.00 | | $135.00 | |

### Authorized Shares

| | | | | |
|---|---|---|---|---|
| Common | 100,000,000 | | 100,000,000 | |

### Shares issued

| | | | | |
|---|---|---|---|---|
| Founders | 1,000,000 | 6% | 1,000,000 | 6% |
| Other execs | 300,000 | 2% | 300,000 | 2% |
| Option plan | 1,600,000 | 10% | 1,600,000 | 10% |
| FF | 650,000 | 4% | 650,000 | 4% |
| Angel | 956,667 | 6% | 956,667 | 6% |
| VC - A | 2,104,444 | 13% | 2,104,444 | 13% |
| VC - B | 3,149,206 | 20% | 3,149,206 | 20% |
| VC - C | 2,970,106 | 18% | 2,970,106 | 18% |
| IPO | 3,350,111 | 21% | 3,350,111 | 21% |
| Total | 16,080,535 | 100% | 16,080,535 | 100% |

### Value of holdings

| | | |
|---|---|---|
| Founders | $35,000,000 | $135,000,000 |
| Other execs | 10,500,000 | 40,500,000 |
| Option plan | 56,000,000 | 216,000,000 |
| FF | 22,750,000 | 87,750,000 |
| Angel | 33,483,333 | 129,150,000 |
| VC - A | 73,655,556 | 284,100,000 |
| VC - B | 110,222,222 | 425,142,857 |
| VC - C | 103,953,704 | 400,964,286 |
| IPO | 117,253,899 | 452,265,038 |
| Capitalization | $562,818,713 | $2,170,872,180 |

### Milestones (at time of funding)

| | | |
|---|---|---|
| Revenue | $45,000,000 | $520,000,000 |
| Net Income | $5,000,000 | $95,000,000 |
| Cash Flow | $7,500,000 | $125,000,000 |
| EPS | $0 | $6 |
| P/E | 71 | 23 |
| Employees | 200 | 1,200 |
| Rev/employee | $225,000 | $433,333 |

105

# Appendix: Glossary Of Terms

**Angel Investor** – an accredited investor who invests in early stage companies. Some angels work alone, others work in groups.

**Accredited Investor** – a person with a liquid net worth of at least $1 million or $200,000 in income for the last two consecutive years.

**Balance Sheet** – statement of assets, liabilities and owner's equity.

**Carry** – term referring to the profits of a venture fund. The limited partners generally take 80%, and the general partners take 20%.

**Cash Flow Statement** – a financial statement showing where cash flowed...literally. The CFS is divided into three parts: operating cash flow, investing cash flow, and financing cash flow. Operating cash flow refers to how much money is generated (or lost) from the operations of the company. This is the measure of how well your company sold what it is supposed to sell, and strips out all superfluous items, such as taxes, interest income or expense, depreciation, and amortization. Investing cash flow refers to how a company spends its money on capital equipment (property, plant, fixtures, etc.), or how it receives cash from the sale of these assets. Financing cash flow shows how much money the company raised (or spent) due to selling (or buying) it's own stock, and/or issuing, servicing and retiring debt.

**Deal** –when referring to a business plan, opportunity or company, the term "deal" is often used.

**Debt** – raising capital by borrowing money.

**Dilution** – you own the same amount of shares in a company, but because more shares have been issued, you own less of the company in percentage terms

**Entrepreneur** – someone with a hole in his head. Why would someone quit a comfy job to chase a dream?

**Equity** – ownership in a company. If you sell stock, you are selling equity.

**Expense Check Entrepreneur** – an original Snow term, typically refers to the blue-blooded MBA who works for a venture funded company, call him/herself an entrepreneur,

**General Partner** – a person at a venture fund who "runs" the fund and makes investments. A general partner may or may not be a limited partner.

**GYHOOYA** – No, not a river in Ohio. It means Get Your Head Out Of Your Ass. In other words: stop kidding yourself, be realistic.

**Idea Stage** – pre revenue. This stage is also called the "ah ha!" stage.

**Income Statement** – financial statement that shows how well a company performed during a period of time.

**Intellectual Property** – the secret sauce of a deal. Most often patented, or at least protected via a trade secret. An idea to write a computer program isn't intellectual property. The actual written code is intellectual property.

**Limited Partner** – the money person behind a fund. This person is called "limited" because he does not actively manage the fund (in other words, he does not make investment decisions).

**Key Number(s)** – the main thing that drives a business. Executives often over saturate themselves with reams of useless information. When you boil it down, managers usually look a just a few discrete numbers. Understand what these key numbers are, focus on these keys, drive these keys, and discount the rest of the information that comes across your desk.

**PIPE** – private investment in public entity. This is when a VC invests in a publicly traded company

**Portfolio Company** – a company that has received investment from a venture capital fund.

**Retained Earnings** – profits

**Run Rate** – the annualized rate of your last month's revenue. For example, if revenues were $83,000 last month, your run rate would be about $1 million ($83,000/month X 12 months)

**Scalability** – the ability to increase sales without having to hire a ton of people.

**Start Up** – a company that is past idea stage, although probably still pre-revenue.

**Term Sheet** – an offer sheet from a VC (or other investor) that describes the terms of the deal. These terms include valuation, how much of the company is being bought, as well as how the investors participate in the operations of the company.

**Trailing Revenue** – the actual revenue of a company for a period of time. Forecasted and otherwise hoped for revenues are not part of trailing revenues.

**Venture Capitalist** – a person who works for a fund that invests in companies that have "critical mass."

If you enjoyed this book, please make sure you check out other books by Bill Snow. And if you didn't like this book, please make sure you check out the other books by Bill Snow, they might be better.

*Venture Capital 101*

*Mergers & Acquisitions For Dummies*

*Networking Is A Curable Condition*

You can contact Bill by email at bill@billsnow.com or visit him at his website www.billsnow.com.

Connect with Bill Snow

Facebook: https://www.facebook.com/BillSnowFanPage

LinkedIn: http://www.linkedin.com/in/billsnow

Twitter: http://www.twitter.com/bill_snow

29852980R00063

Made in the USA
San Bernardino, CA
30 January 2016